G000123368

Studies in Continental Thought

On Translation

JOHN SALLIS

Bloomington & Indianapolis

This book is a publication of

Indiana University Press
601 North Morton Street
Bloomington, IN 47404-3797 USA

http://iupress.indiana.edu

Telephone orders 800-842-6796
Fax orders 812-855-7931
Orders by e-mail iuporder@indiana.edu

The paper used in this publication meets the minimum requirements of American National Standard for Information Sciences—Permanence of Paper for Printed Library Materials, ANSI Z39.48-1984.

Manufactured in the United States of America

Library of Congress Cataloging-in-Publication Data

Sallis, John, date
On translation / John Sallis.
p. cm. — (Studies in Continental thought)
Includes bibliographical references and index.
ISBN 0-253-34156-6 (alk. paper) — ISBN 0-253-21553-6 (pbk. : alk. paper)
1. Translating and interpreting—Philosophy. 2. Semantics (Philosophy) I. Title.
II. Series.
B840 .S25 2002
107′.2—dc21

2002003001

1 2 3 4 5 07 06 05 04 03 02

For Charles Scott
In Honor of Friendship

“Bless thee, Bottom, bless thee! Thou art translated.”

Contents

Preface xi

1. The Dream of Nontranslation 1
2. Scenes of Translation at Large 21
3. Translation and the Force of Words 46
4. Varieties of Untranslatability 112

Index 123

Preface

Translation goes astray.

It happens almost inevitably. It happens both with the word, itself a translation, and with the operation (and product) named *translation.*

Both go, almost inevitably, astray.

To be sure, the word appears stable and its signification well-defined. But nothing could be further from the truth, at least from a certain truth that would consist in coincidence, even in self-sameness. The senses that *translation* would signify and hold in check prove to multiply, spreading and drifting across an extensive, none-too-stable field. Translation itself—though in a sense there is no translation itself—goes likewise astray: gesturing toward the production of sameness (it is called *sameness of meaning* in the classical determination of translation), it cannot but breach the sameness in the foray that must be made into alterity, for instance, into the alterity of another language. It is as if an ineradicable errancy belonged intrinsically to the very truth of translation.

This text, *On Translation,* addresses the theme directly. Yet it does so in such a way as to sustain, almost from the beginning, the doubling of this theme back upon its very thematization; there will be indeed multiple respects in which writing on translation becomes a translating of translation. One could say that translation is intrinsically double, since its movement is always across a differential field. In any case, in *On Translation,* translation becomes a double theme, corresponding to the difference between treating it in its unrestricted spread, as translation at large (Chapter 2), and in its restriction to translation of words (Chapter 3). Treatments of two negative or privative possibilities frame the double treatment of translation: nontranslation, the impossibility of which is almost perpetually countered by a dream (Chapter 1); and untranslatability, which borders on the unspeakable (Chapter 4).

For each of the four themes to which *On Translation* extends, a kind of topology is put into play. Each is referred to a locus, a place, a site, and is interrogated as it takes shape at that site. What drives the interrogation most forcefully is that each of these places is also, in a certain way, noplace, nowhere: what occurs in a dream is nowhere; just as what occurs in the theatre is nowhere, not even in the theatre where it is played; and just as what one sees in a painting or hears in music is nowhere. To say nothing of words, nothing but words, which will at best only open up the difference—one could call it the difference of all differences—between words and the place—the place of all places—where everything comes to pass.

My work on the theme of translation goes back to a lecture presented in 1998 at the Collegium Phaenomenologicum at the invitation of Günter Figal. Subsequently I had opportunities to develop various aspects of this theme in lectures at Trinity College (Connecticut), Tartu University (Estonia), Vassar College, the University of Kansas, and Thammasat University (Bangkok). Some aspects are also developed in a paper, "Hermeneutik der Übersetzung," which appeared in *Hermeneutische Wege: Hans-Georg Gadamer zum Hundertsten*. I am grateful to Nancy Fedrow and Eric Sanday for assistance with production and to my editor and friend Janet Rabinowitch for her generous encouragement and expert advice.

Tübingen
April 2001

On Translation

One The Dream of Nontranslation

What would it mean not to translate? What would it mean to begin thinking beyond all translation? Or, since one will always already have begun, what would it mean to begin again, to launch one's second sailing, beyond all translation? What would it mean to have suspended all translational operations, to have suspended them in the radical sense of having reached a point where even the traces otherwise left by such operations would finally be effaced and rendered ineffective? What would it mean, having reached such a point, to begin again thinking from that point?

If such thinking were possible, if thinking could be situated beyond all translation, it would still not be capable of eluding discourse as such. Neither could it escape entanglement in—to deploy the ancient figure—the fabric of discourse. Its very possibility would require, then, a discourse itself situated beyond translation, a discourse free of translation, a nontranslational discourse.

At least such a bond of thinking to discourse is attested by Kant. Even if there are certain moments in the critical philosophy that seem resistant to such a bond and even though language seldom becomes thematic in Kant's work, it is little wonder that the project of establishing the possibility and limits of pure reason should eventually have come to take up, at least in a supplementary or marginal way, the question of the delimitation of thought by language. It is in a remarkable passage in the *Anthropology* that Kant poses the bond of thinking to language. He begins with the most classical of connections, offering an account that—if one concedes the need, though perhaps not the necessity, of translation—may be rendered thus: "All language is signification of thought, and, on the other hand, the supreme way of signifying thoughts is through language, the greatest means of understanding ourselves and others." Then, most remarkably, he outlines a circulation of speech in and as which thinking comes to pass: "thinking is speaking with ourselves." Kant could hardly have echoed more clearly—whether intentionally or not—Socrates' celebrated declaration to Theaetetus: thinking (διανοεῖσθαι) is "discourse [λόγος] that the soul itself goes through with itself about whatever it is examining. . . . The soul, as it appears to me, in thinking does nothing other than converse [διαλέγεσθαι] with itself, asking and answering itself, and affirming and denying."[1] Kant reinforces the point by adding, parenthetically, an exotic example: "The Indians of Tahiti call thinking: language in the belly." He then rounds out the passage, adding the complementary side of the circuit: "So it is also listening to ourselves inwardly (by reproductive imagination)."[2]

Kant thus attests that thinking is speaking to oneself and inwardly listening, by imagination, to what one says to oneself. Thinking is imaginally listening to oneself as one speaks to oneself; it is speaking to oneself as one imaginally listens to oneself speaking. To the extent that thinking is thus always already drawn into speech, that is, enacted as speech, thoughts will already have been voiced (even if in silence), significations will already have been translated into words. There will always have commenced a translation, not between words within the same language or in different languages, but rather the translation, the circulation, between thought and speech, between meaning and word, that constitutes the very operation of linguistic signification.

If thinking is speaking with oneself, then it will never have outstripped such translation. Thinking will never have been able to begin beyond such translation. In other words, for thinking to begin beyond such translation would mean its collapse into a muteness that could mean nothing at all; incapable of signification, it would have ceased—if thinking is speaking to oneself—even to be thinking. It would have risked a captivation that falls short even of silence, if indeed silence is possible only for one who can speak.

But, granted the bond of thinking to discourse, the confinement of thinking to translation would seem to have followed only because of the excessive drift of the sense of *translation*; once trans-

---

1. Plato, *Theaetetus* 189e–190a.

2. Immanuel Kant, *Anthropologie in Pragmatischer Hinsicht*, in vol. 7 of *Gesammelte Schriften*, ed. Preussische Akademie der Wissenschaft (Berlin, 1902–), 192.

lation is extended to cover the very operation of signification as such, it will contaminate, as it were, whatever is bound to discourse. On the other hand, one may, with some legitimacy no doubt, insist on limiting the drift of translation, on restricting the sense of the word such that it applies only to certain linkages between signifiers in different languages and perhaps also between signifiers in a single language. With this limit in place, one could then propose a point of nontranslation, a zero-degree point where discourse would contract into a purely monolingual and nonmetaphorical operation (assuming that the word *metaphorical* can appropriately—or even by a certain drift—cover all cases of translation within a single language). It is in such a contracted discourse that thinking would venture—were it possible—beyond translation. Set at the point of nontranslation, speaking to oneself in the pure discourse that becomes possible only at this point, one's thinking would—were such possible—launch itself anew. No longer distracted by diversions from meaning as such, no longer called upon to detour through a speech even slightly deviant, thinking in this pure discourse could set about forming its encyclopedia. Somewhat as the ancient Babylonians, gifted with a common language, undisturbed by any foreign tongue—or rather, lip, as the Hebrew says, broaching metaphor or rather metonymy in the very name of discourse—set about to build—translating this nontranslation—"a city and a tower with its top in the sky."[3]

Genesis tells of how Yahweh came down to mix up their language so that they could no longer understand one another, of how he scattered them over the face of the earth, bringing to an end that project so monumental that Hegel took it to mark the beginning of architecture. The Genesis story concludes by telling of the name given to this place where the mixing up of languages occurred. The name *Babel*, the proper name that ought properly to be untranslatable like other proper names, is translated by confusion into what we translate as the common noun *confusion*. The confusion of tongues/lips imposes the necessity of translation. It imposes also a certain impossibility of translation, or, more precisely,

3. Genesis 11:4.

a limit that prevents translation from overcoming the mutual disjointedness of languages and thereby reclaiming in effect the common language, compensating without residue for the confusion of tongues.[4]

Is the thinking that would take place as pure discourse beyond all translation destined to be undone by a corresponding confusion? Is it, too, properly—and so also improperly—named *Babel*? Is it, too, inevitably to be scattered, speaking to itself in metaphors and in foreign tongues, submitted to the necessity of translation but also to the impossibility of recovering through translation what seemed a point of nontranslation? And, if thinking thus proves incapable of sustaining its conversation with itself otherwise than by an engagement in translation that opens it to what is foreign, does this mean that the prospect of nontranslation disappears entirely? Or, even against mounting odds, even in the face of apparent impossibility—or rather, because of this—does one still dream of nontranslation?

Still? Even against mounting odds? Against, on the one hand, theoretical odds? Consider the purview that has opened on the words that, in the modern European languages, convey the traditionally basic philosophical concepts and principles, regardless of whether they are taken over and renewed or put in question and displaced in their sense. These words (*substance, accident, subject, cause, essence,* etc.) are preponderantly translations, if not simply transliterations, of Latin philosophical terms. Though one can of course undertake to redetermine the sense of such words so as, in the end, to render the translational traces no longer effective, there is no telling how widely the attempt to do so would have to venture in redetermining words whose values are so thoroughly interrelated among themselves and in the language as a whole; neither, then, can there be much assurance of reaching the end. Even if, instead of trying to neutralize the translation from Latin, one were to hold back from this translation, attempting—without translating back from one's own language—to write philosophically in

4. See my discussion in "Babylonian Captivity," *Research in Phenomenology* 22 (1992): 23–31. Also Jacques Derrida, "Des Tours de Babel," in *Psyché: Inventions de l'autre* (Paris: Galilée, 1987), 203–35.

Latin, as was still possible in eighteenth-century Germany, one's text would still be compromised by translation, still bearing, as it would, traces of the translation from Greek. The compromise would be all the greater as ever more decisiveness came to be accorded to the translation of Greek philosophical words into the Latin terms that one would either seek to renew—most likely in vain—or else simply carry over into the modern languages. In recent engagements with Greek thought, there is much—the mounting odds—to urge according the utmost decisiveness to this translation. Beginning with Heidegger's work on the Greeks, it has become increasingly evident that the translation of Greek philosophical words into Latin terms was anything but a series of substitutions of one signifier for another over against a selfsame, persistent meaning that both equally would signify. Even if one were to insist on a certain reticence, on suspending any totalizing evaluation, there is still no denying the decisiveness of the transition in which philosophy came to be written in Latin rather than Greek. That the translation of ὑποκείμενον into *subiectum* was a transformation of sense is confirmed perhaps most definitively by the decisive shift that the very site named by the word eventually underwent so as to allow the word finally to name what modern philosophy calls the subject. One could—without exaggeration—speak of an abysmal leap rather than a transition in the case of the translation of χώρα, as this word (that borders on not being a word) was determined in the *Timaeus*, its translation by Chalcidius as *locus* (hence into English by Thomas Taylor as *place*). This leap, not over but away from the abyss, this retreat before the abyss, named (insofar as it can be named) by χώρα, effected a transformation not just of sense but rather of the very sense of sense.

These examples, which bear upon the very possibility and operation of exemplarity, could be multiplied so as to show again and again that any history of translation is something quite other than a story of a series of signifiers successively taking over the function of signifying one and the same signification. It is precisely because of the density, manifoldness, and complications of such histories that access to Greek thought requires the careful and persistent work of separating the multiple folds and breaking up the sediment of translational operations. Only by way of a countertranslating that translates back from one's own language to Greek without translating one's own language back into—back upon—the Greek can one, as Heidegger proposed, translate Aristotle back into Greek, gaining an access to the Greek text that, far from being independent of translation, would depend on an ever renewed translational—or countertranslational—strategy that could hardly be more demanding.

In no case, it seems, could one reach a point either of nontranslation or of such translation/countertranslation as could effectively master the disjunction between languages so as to cancel the effects of translation and effectively restore perfectly conjoined points of nontranslation. And yet, in the face of such apparent impossibility, even against such mounting odds, does one still dream of nontranslation?

Still? Even against mounting odds on the practical side? Against, for instance, the mounting odds accumulating around the phenomenon called—and constituted—by the name *globalization*? Consider that the very name designates a kind of unlimited translation, translation of everything across all borders. Rather than effacing these borders, globalization only renders them permeable; if nothing else does so, the persistence of linguistic differences guarantees that borders, however permeable, remain and remain effective. As since Babel, translation remains necessary and yet in a sense impossible, in the sense that its success can never consist in effacing the borders and establishing a virtual reign of nontranslation. In the wake of globalization, whether one is drawn along or remains resistant, one is translated ever more into translation, if not between languages then at least in the negotiations between cultures that take place with regard to everything that crosses the borders, whether artworks or customs or agricultural products. In this very connection there arises the danger of a certain accommodation in which one would be prone to fail to recognize the necessity and the effects of translation. A certain complicity between the spread of English almost everywhere and the dream of nontranslation threatens to render translational effects and the borders to which they attest less and less perceptible. And yet, the threat has not gone simply unrecognized as the odds have mounted against the assumption that speaking English, speaking even in the style and idiom of an American, is speaking without translation.

Yet the dream, it seems, persists against all odds. Its sequences unfold, flowing into one another yet without ever quite cohering. The dream continues, as in every case, in a way that is neither simply indifferent to one's participation nor, on the other hand, merely dependent on one's conscious and deliberate intention. It flows on, engendering hope, renewing ever again the very will that, even if by a barely decipherable mechanism, it fulfills. Even as, in what as waking life one would contrast with the dream, one confronts and perhaps even acknowledges the impossibility of nontranslation, the dream persists and flows over into waking life, even in a sense takes over the day, instills a certain madness of the day, this daydream that is confinable neither just to the night nor just to the day.

The dream of nontranslation is no more transparent than in most other cases. What the dream is about is not manifest in the dream. What is manifest, what in this sense one actually dreams about, is something else the formation of which must be exposed by an appropriate analysis in order to bring to light what the dream is—as one will say—truly about, its latent content. Certain manifest contents suggest themselves: for instance (and it is most likely not just an instance), the contents of dreams of complete mastery, of such dreams as those that thoroughly inform the drive of technology. But only by way of a kind of psychoanalysis (one twisted free of the theoretical constraints that, for all its force, limit Freud's work) could one expose, beneath the technological mastery manifestly dreamed of, the operation of a will to nontranslation.

Thus does psychoanalysis have a bearing on nontranslation, just as, conversely, the concept or schema of translation bears on the very articulation of the framework of psychoanalysis. Referring to the latent and manifest dream-contents, respectively, as the dream-thoughts and the dream-content, Freud writes: "The dream-thoughts and the dream-content lie before us like two presentations [*Darstellungen*] of the same content in two different languages, or rather, the dream-content appears to us as a translation

[*Übertragung*] of the dream-thoughts into another mode of expression, and we are supposed to get to know its signs and its laws of construction by comparing the original and the translation. . . . The dream-content is given, as it were, in pictographic script whose signs are to be translated [*übertragen*] individually into the language of the dream-thoughts."[5] In short, the production of the dream-content is a translating of the dream-thoughts, and the task of psychoanalysis is to countertranslate from the language of the dream-content back into that of the dream-thoughts. Or rather, this countertranslating is what Freud in later texts calls the practical task of psychoanalysis, in distinction from the theoretical task of explaining the process—the dream-work—by which the dream-thoughts come to be translated into the dream-content.[6] Freud insists that the interpretation of a dream, that is, the countertranslating of manifest into latent content, can never be declared finished and in itself complete: "actually one is never certain of having completely interpreted a dream; even when the solution seems satisfying and without gaps, it remains always possible for a further meaning to announce itself through the same dream."[7] Thus countertranslation can never be assured of having decisively undone all that translation would have accomplished; it can never be certain of having arrived at a point of nontranslation. The possibility always remains that what seems simply a dream-thought may prove to be a still unrecognized translation, the meaning of which—the concealed dream-thought behind which—has still to be deciphered. Even in the analysis of the dream of nontranslation, there would be no assurance of ever having reached a point of nontranslation. Regressing from the content, for instance, of dreams of complete mastery, countertranslation could never itself master the latent content exposed, could never display that

5. Sigmund Freud, *Die Traumdeutung*, vol. 2 of *Studienausgabe* (Frankfurt a.M.: S. Fischer, 2000), 280.

6. *Neue Folge der Vorlesungen zur Einführung in die Psychoanalyse*, in vol. 1 of *Studienausgabe*, 453. See my discussion of the hermeneutics of the resulting circularity in "The Logic and Illogic of the Dream-Work," in *Freud's Unconscious Ontology*, ed. Jon Mills, forthcoming.

7. Freud, *Die Traumdeutung*, 282.

content as a signification free of all translational effects. Not even the dream-thought of nontranslation could be secured at a point of nontranslation. To say nothing of the further complication, the further translation, involved in the very production of the dream-thoughts: for, granted Freud's thesis regarding the dream as wish-fulfillment, the production of the dream-thoughts would translate a certain determinate will—would translate it into the dream-thoughts—and, through the fulfillment achieved in the dream, would translate that will, as it were, back to itself.

There are certain rare cases in which no disguise intervenes.[8] In these cases the dream-thoughts are not submitted to a distortion productive of another content that would serve to conceal the dream-thoughts themselves. Rather, in these cases what one actually dreams about coincides with what the dream is—as one will say—truly about.

While still in his youth Leibniz came upon the thought of a kind of universal alphabet of human knowledge. In *De Arte Combinatoria*, published in 1666, he proposes to search for this universal alphabet, which, employing mathematical signs, not only would found all discovery and judgment but also would allow communication with others independently of their particular word-language. The text from 1677 generally known as *Foundations of a Universal Characteristic*[9] (though untitled in the original) is perhaps most explicit: Leibniz writes of "a kind of language or universal characteristic in which all concepts and things would be brought into the proper order and with the aid of which it would become possible for various peoples to communicate their feelings and thoughts and to read in their own language what another has written in his language." Such a language—for which "one must go beyond words" —would compensate definitively for the disorder, the deviations and noncorrespondences, of word-languages, and it would introduce a reign of unlimited communication, eliminating both the necessity of translation and the limits that prevent its success from in effect canceling that necessity. Through the introduction of such

8. See ibid., 136–46.

9. G. W. Leibniz, *Die philosophischen Schriften*, ed. C. J. Gerhardt (Hildesheim: Georg Olms, 1965), 7:184ff.

a language, translation—both as the metaphorical transfer that would compensate for the deviations and noncorrespondences in a language and as transferal from one language to another—would be replaced by operations of analysis and synthesis: "Through the connection of its letters and the analysis of the words composed from them [words that would be beyond word, replaced by mathematical signs] everything else could be discovered and judged." What is perhaps most remarkable about this text is that it remains purely a proposal, that it offers not the slightest element of such a language, though Leibniz assures his readers that "it would not require any more work than that currently applied to encyclopedias"; he is confident that the work needed for this new encyclopedia, as one could call it, the true encyclopedia that would involve and require no translation, will require no more than five years. Leibniz even reveals the colonialism that is implicated—as in the Genesis story—with the claim to a universal language: "if this language is introduced by the missionaries, then also the true religion, which is most perfectly unifiable with reason, will be established on firm ground." And yet, this dream of nontranslation, its sequence unfolding from the vision of universal communication on through the prospect of converting savages to the true religion, can persist as such only by concealing something, so that even in this seemingly most transparent dream of nontranslation distortion and disguise are not entirely lacking. What must remain disguised is that, while excluded within this universal language, translation would nonetheless be required between this language and the word-languages that humans speak and that—perhaps indefinitely, in any case well beyond the five years that writing the true encyclopedia would require—they will continue to speak. If all peoples are "to read in their own language what another has written in his language," then translation must take place between the universal language (legible to all) and each people's own language.[10]

---

10. In the development of formal logic along lines anticipated by Leibniz's proposal, the character of the formalizing transferal from so-called natural languages to a formal system has been a theme of recurrent debate. A recent discussion by Robert Wardy appeals to a warning by Christopher Kirwan: "'one

Leibniz not only envisaged a virtual end of translation but also, at quite a different level, assigned a positive, critical function to translation between certain existing languages. In 1670, only four years after *De Arte Combinatoria* announced for the first time the project of universal language, Leibniz prepared an edition of a work by the Italian humanist Marius Nizolius that had first appeared in 1553 under the title *On the True Principles of Philosophy, against Pseudo-Philosophers;* for this edition Leibniz wrote an Introduction, referred to as "On the Philosophical Style of Nizolius."[11] It is in this Introduction that he discusses the critical function that translation is capable of performing. The discussion occurs in the context of a broad critical rejection of Scholasticism, though, characteristically and in distinction from most such critics of the time, Leibniz sets apart those philosophers of sound and useful learning "who draw from the springs of Aristotle and the ancients rather than from the cisterns of the Scholastics." Leibniz's point of departure is provided by Nizolius' insistence that whatever cannot be named in the vernacular is to be regarded as nonexistent, fictitious, and useless. Leibniz endorses Nizolius' position in this respect: whatever cannot be explained in popular terms, in the words of some living and popular language, is nothing and should be exorcised from philosophy unless it is something that can be known by immediate sense experience. Leibniz thus attributes the

---

might be tempted to think of the whole process of formalising as a kind of translation from words into symbols; but because the steps in it do not have to preserve sameness of meaning they are translations of a special kind, and in particular schematising is far from coming under the ordinary idea of translating.'" Wardy himself writes: "But crucially, I do not regard any such formal representations as *translations* of 'natural' sentences. Why would one think in the first place that depicting 'all animals are mortal' as '('∀x)(Ax ⊃ Mx)' is on all fours with translating it as 'omnia animalia sunt mortalia'?" Taking a more unqualifiedly negative position even than Kirwan, he goes on to refer to "the delusive conception of 'translation' into a formal system" (Robert Wardy, *Aristotle in China: Language, Categories and Translation* [Cambridge: Cambridge University Press, 2000], 35–37).

11. Leibniz, *Die Philosophischen Schriften,* 4:138–76. English citations are adapted from Leibniz, *Philosophical Papers and Letters,* ed. Leroy E. Loemker (Dordrecht: Reidel, 1969), 121–30.

persistence of the exaggerated Scholastic style of philosophy in Germany to the failure to progress from Latin to German. In contrast to their counterparts in England and France, German philosophers of the time had hardly even begun to cultivate philosophy in their own tongue. In Leibniz's words, translated from the Latin in which he himself wrote: "In Germany the Scholastic philosophy is more firmly established because, among other reasons, a late start was made in philosophizing in German, and even now we have hardly made an adequate beginning." What is especially lacking in German philosophy is the exercise of the critical function that translation of Latin philosophical terms into the popular language can perform, the function of testing and explaining—or in some cases exorcising—the terms of the Latin discourse. Though in Germany this critical function has hardly begun to be carried out, Leibniz privileges the German language in this regard: "But I venture to say that no European language is better suited than German for this testing and examination of philosophical doctrines by a living tongue." The privilege accorded to German is the result of its remoteness from Latin. Whereas "many terms of Scholastic philosophy have been retained in some way in French translation," German is so removed from Latin that it will not accept such terms. Whatever would be translated from Latin into German would also, because of the extreme difference, be submitted to a critical test, more critical than in the case of Latinate languages. Leibniz expresses no concern that such translation might result in significational loss; on the contrary, he seems fully confident of the inevitable gain—if not in signification, then at least in clarity.

One would presume that this critical function of translation would indeed have been tacitly operative as Leibniz continued to write largely in Latin and in French. On the other hand, there are German texts in which he explicitly begins the task of translating the Latin philosophical vocabulary into German. In these texts he not only writes in German but skillfully introduces German terms to replace those of Latin Scholasticism, for instance, *Selbstbestand* for *substantia* and *Unwesen* for *materia*.[12] Yet the dream persists; its

12. See Leibniz, *Philosophical Papers and Letters*, 367.

thought, nontranslation, will be announced more definitively a few years later in *Foundations of a Universal Characteristic*. As long as the dream persists, the labor of translating Latin philosophical terms into German can only be—can only have been—regarded as preparatory to the institution of the universal language, as critical, clarifying work in anticipation of the time—Leibniz thought it only a few years hence—when philosophy would be in a position to put aside every particular language, replacing them with a universal characteristic perfectly matched with thought as such.

Even with Kant, who rarely addresses the theme,[13] the dream

---

13. One text in which this theme does arise, though briefly, is a short piece from 1785 entitled *On the Injustice of Counterfeiting Books*. In this text Kant makes his case against counterfeiting books by insisting on the distinction between a work (*Werk*) and an act (*Handlung*); indeed, as if to stabilize the distinction and protect it from such erosion as living and popular language might produce, Kant appeals to—translates back into—Latin, that is, he translates the distinction as that between *opus* and *opera*. Kant grants that an artwork, because it is an *opus* and not an *opera*, may be copied by anyone who has rightfully acquired it and without the consent or mention of the producer; the work and its copies may be put up for sale without the original producer's having any right to complain of interference in his affairs. But it is otherwise with the writing of another. In Kant's words: "The writing of another is the speech of a person (*opera*); and whoever publishes it can speak to the public only in the name of this other and can say nothing more of himself than that the author makes the following speech through him (*Impensis Bibliopolae*)," Kant again, it seems, with the parenthesized words seeking to stabilize the meaning by translation back into Latin. The reason, then, that books, unlike artworks, are not to be imitated, counterfeited, is that they are not works (*opera*) but rather acts (*Handlungen*) (*operae*), which can have their existence only in a person, which belong therefore inalienably to the person of the author, who has thus an inalienable right always to speak *himself* through every other that puts forth the book. On the other hand, if a book is abridged, augmented, or retouched, then it would be wrong to put it forth in the name of the author; presenting the alterations in the proper name of the editor would not be counterfeit. It is likewise, says Kant, with translation: "Translation into another language cannot be taken to be counterfeit; for it is not the same speech of the author, though the thoughts may be exactly the same" (*Von der Unrechtmässigkeit des Büchernachdrucks*, in vol. 8 of *Gesammelte Schriften*, 86f.). Kant does not pursue this question of translation further. He does not, for instance, consider whether it would be imperative to include the name of the original author along with that of the translator, as indeed one might well suppose on the ground that thinking is no less act (*opera*) than is speech. Is one's own thought

of nontranslation persists virtually without disguise, though limited to a very specific connection. The connection is the same as that addressed by Leibniz in his Introduction to Nizolius' work, namely, that between Latin (the dead and scholarly language) and living and popular languages. Yet the translation from the former to the latter, which to Leibniz constituted a critical gain, appeared to Kant to produce a certain loss that, in a certain area at least, needed to be forestalled or reversed. In the establishing of a bulwark against certain effects within living and popular languages, the dream of nontranslation, at least one brief sequence, is renewed.

The pertinent discussion is linked to what Kant writes in the *Critique of Judgment* about the role of genius in art: not only that genius gives the rule to art but also that this talent, as a natural gift (*Naturgabe*), is that through which nature gives the rule to art. A decisive consequence is that the rule issuing from this double giving (nature's endowment to the artist, which, in turn, gives the rule to art) cannot be encapsulated in a formula that could then serve as a precept for judging and for producing artworks. All that is available are models, which other artists may imitate in testing their own talents. Though Kant grants that it is difficult to explain how such imitation (*Nachahmung*) is possible, he insists that models to be thus imitated are the only means of transmitting an artist's ideas to posterity. Kant adds a rigorous requirement in the area of the arts of speech: "in these arts only those models can become classical that are written in the ancient, dead languages, now preserved only as scholarly languages."[14] The basis for this requirement is explained in a note added to another, somewhat parallel passage in which Kant refers to models through imitation of which one can manifest, though certainly not acquire, taste. The note reads: "Models of taste in the arts of speech must be composed in a dead and scholarly language: dead, so that it will not have to undergo the *changes* that inevitably affect living ones, whereby noble

---

not still in some measure one's own even when it is expressed in another voice, even in a foreign voice? Or does the requirement that thought be enacted as speech entail a connection so intimate that the thought, too, would be alienated in being expressed in an alien voice?

14. Kant, *Kritik der Urteilskraft*, in vol. 5 of *Gesammelte Schriften*, §47.

expressions become flat, familiar ones archaic, and newly created ones enter into circulation for only a short while; scholarly, so that it will have a grammar that is not subject to the whims of fashion but *has* its own unchangeable rule."[15] At least in the arts of speech, in the models to be imitated in poetry and oratory, the living and popular character of current languages is counterproductive. For such models dead, scholarly languages that are spoken natively by no one are superior.

This reversion to the dead and scholarly language, even if only within a very limited area, is in effect a retreat before a kind of translation that occurs, not between languages, but within a language. It is a kind of diachronic translation that living and popular languages undergo as if in and of themselves. It is a translation in which semantic elements undergo displacement ("whereby noble expressions become flat, familiar ones archaic, and newly created ones enter into circulation for only a short while"), as also do syntactical rules ("a grammar . . . subject to the whims of fashion"). Models of taste in the arts of speech can endure only by being withdrawn from this translation at work in all living and popular languages, only by being composed in a dead and scholarly language.

Such is, then, the reversal that Kant, writing in German, proposes. Whatever advantages might—at least within this very limited area—be gained by translation to German (as Leibniz, writing in Latin, proposed) seem completely outweighed by the gain in defense against the uncontrollable translation at work in all living and popular languages.

This very translation, the uncontrollable change within any living language, is one of the focal points of Benjamin's reflection in "The Task of the Translator." But for Benjamin the transformation within living languages is not something that calls for defense and reversion but rather is the expression of the afterlife of an original work, the afterlife for which the translations of the work are primary vehicles. In its translation into another language, a work lives on. Surviving is undergoing transformation and renewal: "There

15. Ibid., §17.

is a further ripening [*Nachreife*] even of words with fixed meaning. What may in the author's time have been the tendency of his poetic language can later be worn out; immanent tendencies can arise anew from what has taken shape. What once sounded fresh can later sound hackneyed; what at the time sounded normal can later sound archaic."[16] For Benjamin recognition of these uncontrollable transformations, far from prescribing retreat and defense, suggests that translation cannot be determined on the basis of a static likeness to the original. Recognition of these transformations points thus to the redetermination that Benjamin undertakes of the task of the translator.

But if translation from the dead and scholarly languages to and into German exposes what is written to the uncontrollable transformations at work in every living and popular language, it also can bring about an opening to what has been written, to what was once written in the ancient, classical languages and has retained, if only covertly, a certain force as origin of Western thought. To attempt to bring about such an opening is what Hegel proposed when, in a letter written in 1805 to the classicist J. H. Voss, the translator of Homer into German, he said of his own endeavor that he wished "to try to teach philosophy to speak German."[17] The opening to the ancients would not be a matter primarily of translating oneself back to the ancients but rather of a return to self through which the ancients would be appropriated. Hegel explains why such translation is the "greatest gift that can be made to a people": "For a people remains barbarian and does not view what is excellent within the range of its acquaintance as its own true property so long as it does not come to know it in its own language." It was precisely for the sake of such appropriation of the wealth of significations informing the works of the ancients that Hegel took up and extended in the direction of Greek antiquity the program of translation into German that Leibniz had already broached with critical intent.

---

16. Walter Benjamin, "Die Aufgabe des Übersetzers," in *Illuminationen* (*Ausgewählte Schriften 1*) (Frankfurt a.M.: Suhrkamp, 1977), 53–54.

17. *Briefe von und an Hegel*, ed. J. Hoffmeister (Hamburg: Felix Meiner, 1952), 1:99f. (#55).

Across all the differences, abysmal though they be, there is a certain solidarity between Heidegger and Hegel as regards translation and tradition. In *The Principle of Reason* Heidegger writes about translations that at the appropriate time render a work of poetry (*Dichten*) or of thinking. In such cases, says Heidegger, translation is not only interpretation but *Überlieferung*, tradition in the sense of handing-down (not just what is handed down, say, in the sense of the "content" of tradition, but the handing-down itself, that by which the "content" of tradition gets handed down from one epoch to another). As such, translation "belongs to the innermost movement of history."[18] Still further: "An essential translation corresponds [*entspricht*] . . . to the way in which a language speaks in the sending of being [*wie im Geschick des Seins eine Sprach spricht*]." It is because such translations inscribe responsively the saying within the sending of being (the saying of being as ἰδέα, as ἐνέργεια, as *actualitas*, . . . as will to power) that they belong to the innermost movement of history, constituting nodal points, points of jointure, where tradition (handing down from the sending of being) takes place. This is the connection in which to consider Heidegger's preoccupation with the transformation wrought by the translation from Greek to Latin: "Roman thought takes over the Greek words [*die griechische Wörter*] without a corresponding, equally originary experience of what they say, without the Greek word [*ohne das griechische Wort*]."[19] This translation inscribes a muted saying, that of a sending that also decisively withholds. Because it is not just momentous but decisively epochal, Heidegger declares, in words otherwise astonishing: "The groundlessness of Western thought begins with this translation."

Yet such translational inscription cannot be only a matter of appropriation. Certainly not in the sense proposed by Hegel: in what Heidegger delimits as the end of philosophy, such appropriation will already have occurred, indeed with such force that, short of the most radical measures, we—the *we* who belong to this closure —will continue indefinitely circulating within the system of sig-

---

18. Martin Heidegger, *Der Satz vom Grund* (Pfullingen: Neske, 1957), 164.

19. Heidegger, "Der Ursprung des Kunstwerkes," in *Holzwege*, vol. 5 of *Gesamtausgabe* (Frankfurt a.M.: Vittorio Klostermann, 1977).

nifications that translation will have made our own. What, then, are the radical measures needed? In the course of a discussion of how such fundamental words as ὄν and εἶναι are to be understood, Heidegger declares precisely what measures are needed: "that, instead of merely bringing the Greek words into words belonging to the German language, we ourselves pass over from our side into the Greek linguistic domain . . . of ὄν and εἶναι."[20] It is not only a matter of taking over from the Greeks what they have thought and said but of setting ourselves back into the Greek, into the domain from which Greek thinking and saying issued. In his lecture course *Parmenides*, in connection with a discussion of the translation of ἀλήθεια as *Unverborgenheit*, Heidegger explains the translation that in this connection is required of us as translators: "If we merely replace the Greek ἀλήθεια with the German '*Unverborgenheit*,' we are not yet translating. That happens only when the translating word '*Unverborgenheit*' *trans*lates us into the domain and mode of experience from out of which the Greeks and in the present case the originary thinker Parmenides said the word ἀλήθεια."[21] The task of the translator is a certain abandonment, as is bespoken by the translation within the word *Aufgabe* itself. The task of the translator is, first of all, to be translated into the domain in which what is to be translated was originarily said.

Yet these translations—translations of Greek by translation back into Greek—are not the only ones belonging to thinking. Heidegger observes that "we continually translate also our own language, our native language, into its own words."[22] He declares even that "translation of one's own language into its ownmost word" is more difficult than translating from another language. In any case he insists that the speaking in which thinking is enacted "is in itself a translating," that in it "an originary translating holds sway." Thus does Heidegger declare the utterly translational character of thinking; in its various modes and directions translation is always operative, and there is no thinking beyond translation. In the fab-

20. Heidegger, *Was Heisst Denken?* (Tübingen: Max Niemeyer, 1954), 138.

21. Heidegger, *Parmenides*, vol. 54 of *Gesamtausgabe* (Frankfurt a.M.: Vittorio Klostermann, 1982), 16.

22. Ibid., 17–18.

ric of discourse in which thinking enacts itself, there is not a single thread that has not been spun and woven by translation. Thus dissolving the dream, Heidegger proclaims a reign of translation.

The reign of translation is a disjointed gathering that not only is to be thought but also can be played out in dramatic poetry, in the theatre. It is played out with an appropriateness that one could most likely never have imagined possible in *A Midsummer Night's Dream.*[23] What the play presents is, above all, a dream of translation, a dream that is itself enacted as a translation from Athens to the nearby wood, a dream in which the four lovers, thus translated, undergo the effects of certain translations and countertranslations of fancies, a dream in which simple mechanicals are translated into actors, and one of them, declared and shown to have been even monstrously translated, is in turn installed in the domain of the fairy queen, that is, translated from the world of humans (in and from the gross form he has assumed) into the tiny world of the fairies. As Titania extends her promise to him, she summons those slight creatures who serve her:

> Therefore go with me.
> I'll give thee fairies to attend on thee;
> And they shall fetch thee jewels from the deep,
> And sing, while thou on pressed flowers dost sleep:
> And I will purge thy mortal grossness so,
> That thou shalt like an airy spirit go.
> Peaseblossom! Cobweb! Moth! and Mustardseed!
> (III.i.149–55)

The play is a dream, then, of translation and countertranslation. It is played out as a gathering of translations, which, however much they seem, with the return to Athens, to have been no more than

> . . . the fierce vexation of a dream[,]
> (IV.i.68)

23. Citations from William Shakespeare, *A Midsummer Night's Dream*, are from the Arden text edited by Harold F. Brooks (London: Routledge, 1979).

nonetheless leave a certain disjointure. They leave, most notably, a disjointure of that which disjoints everything (even eventually from itself): time itself. For if one counts the days or nights of the dream, it turns out that at least one has been utterly dreamed away, the four days spoken of at the outset of the play having been thus spanned by three days.[24] Disjointing time from itself, the play—in other respects too—forestalls resolution into nontranslation, remains to the very end a play of translation.

---

24. At the outset of the play Hippolyta says:

> Four days will quickly steep themselves in night;
> Four nights will quickly dream away the time.
>
> (I.i.7–8)

This is in a sense just what happens: the time is dreamed away, but *not* in *four* nights, not in the *four* days that will steep themselves in night. A count of the days comes up short. On the first day Hermia, Lysander, and Demetrius appear at Theseus' court, and Egeus proclaims his interdiction. Lysander and Hermia plan to flee "tomorrow night" (I.i.164; I.i.209). Thus, the second day is the one on the night of which they flee and the various nocturnal happenings take place in the wood (see, e.g., the reference to "yonder Venus" [III.ii.61]), all four lovers finally lying asleep on the ground. On the third day they are awakened; it is the day of the new moon, the day on which the wedding of Theseus and Hippolyta takes place.

A similar contraction seems to occur in Act V, in which the play within the play allows the time to be dreamed away. At the beginning Theseus refers to

> this long age of three hours
>
> (V.i.33)

that has to be worn away before bedtime. Along with Theseus and his company, we too, the spectators of the play itself, watch the play within the play that is to help pass the time. One thing is certain: "Pyramus and Thisbe" does not last for three hours. Yet in his last speech immediately following the play, Theseus proclaims:

> The iron tongue of midnight hath told twelve.
> Lovers, to bed. . . .
> . . . .
> This palpable-gross play hath well beguil'd
> The heavy gait of night. Sweet friends, to bed.
>
> (V.i.349–50, 353–54)

Two *Scenes of Translation at Large*

Writing on translation inevitably becomes entangled. For nothing quite suffices to keep such writing from getting mixed up with what is written about. Even if one touches ever so lightly on translation, one will not be able to prevent a certain adherence of translation to the discourse on translation. Nothing can quite facilitate producing a discourse on translation that would remain entirely distinct from translation. Writing on translation cannot but get entangled in translation; inevitably it gets caught up in translating translation and to this extent cannot but take for granted precisely that which the discourse would as such first delimit. Even simply to explain what translation is, simply to interpret the meaning of the word—assuming such simple explanation and interpretation to be possible—is, in a sense, in a primary sense of the word, to translate. There are no means by which to delimit a discourse on translation that would be entirely free of translation. There are no means by which to limit, as it were, the contamination of such discourse by translation.

To venture a discourse on translation is thus to invite complication as such. Translation insinuates itself in discourse on translation: most directly perhaps when such discourse is made to engage in translating *translation*, translating it in the sense of transposing it into other words, explicating or explaining it. To say nothing of the fact that *translation*—the word, which, following a familiar schema, one will presume to distinguish from the thing itself and from its meaning—is itself a translation mediated by an extended and complex history. This history is not simply constituted by a sequence of words by which an invariant meaning would be preserved and reexpressed in successive languages. Not only is the semantic field of the word bound up with its translation, but, still more decisively, both word and translation are fundamentally engaged with the metaphysical determination of language as such and with its development beyond—yet on the basis of—the Greek beginning. As soon as one utters the word *translation*, one has already resumed a history of translation and installed what one would say within the parameters of that history.

Translation is performative. Or at least under a certain provocation the word can be induced to perform what it says. With only the slightest energizing of its polysemy, its slippage between various meanings will come into play, its slippage across a remarkably extensive field of meanings. By way of this slippage, the word undergoes what also it says. In other words—and here already I have begun to translate, here already translation insinuates itself into the discourse on translation, reducing the separation between saying and said—in other words, translating into other words, the word *translation* can thus be induced to undergo translation from one meaning to another across an extensive semantic field. In other words—again I am translating—once its polysemy is energized, *translation* is released into a play of translation and endowed with a semantic mobility that will not prove readily controllable.

One could say that *translation* is like a translation, that in its performance the word resembles especially a not very good translation. Its slippage between various meanings is similar to that by which a not very good translation typically shifts between disparate words or phrases in a less than successful effort to render a semantically unified original text. In reading such a translation, one reaches a certain point of intolerance with respect to the indecisive semantic shifts, and then, if one has the competence to do so, one turns to the original in order to determine more precisely what is meant. For the word *translation* there is also a kind of original. Some measure can be gained against the word's otherwise indetermining mobility by turning back to that original, by untranslating or countertranslating *translation* back across its history.

The range of the word *translation* is enormous. One can speak of translating words and sentences belonging to one language into the corresponding words and sentences of another language. Yet one can also speak of translating ideas into action, hence of translation as mediating the difference between θεωρία and πρᾶξις. There would seem to be virtually no limit to the extension of which the word, by generalization, is capable. From its more limited senses it readily slides toward the unlimited sense of movement or change across some kind of interval—that is (again, as almost always, I am translating), it slides toward signifying transition as such.

This most general, almost unlimitedly general, signification is guaranteed by the word's etymology. The word derives, by way of the Middle English *translaten*, from the Latin *translatus*, which was used as the past participle of *transfero*. Composed from the roots *trans* (across) and *fero* (carry, bear), *transfero* is preserved in the modern English *transfer*. Thus regarded, to translate is to transfer, to carry or bear across some interval. In Latin a *translator* is one who carries something over, a transferer. One of the specific things that can be transferred is meaning, as when the meaning of one word is transferred to another. If those words belong to different languages, then there is translation in the specific sense of translating something in one language into the words of another language. But there can also be such translation, such transfer of meaning, within the same language, for example, between what are called synonyms.

Thus Jakobson differentiates between interlingual translation, which consists in "an interpretation of verbal signs by means of some other language," and intralingual translation, which is "an interpretation of verbal signs by means of other signs of the same language." And though restricting translation to systems of signs and to translation of verbal signs, thus reducing its generality considerably, Jakobson does at least grant also a third kind of translation more extensive that the other two; this third kind, termed intersemiotic translation, consists in "an interpretation of verbal signs by means of signs of nonverbal sign systems."[1]

Under certain conditions translation within the same language produces what is called a metaphor. Thus the Latin noun *translatio* means not only transfer but also metaphor or figure.[2] Indeed the

1. Roman Jakobson, *Language in Literature*, ed. Krystyna Pomorska and Stephen Rudy (Cambridge, Mass.: Harvard University Press, 1987), 429.

2. Thus Cicero writes of *translatio*, by which he translates μεταφορά: "*Translatio* occurs when a word applying to one thing is transferred to another because the

two words *translation* and *metaphor* are, etymologically considered, virtually identical. Or rather, *translation* is linked to *metaphor* by way of the ancient translation of μεταφέρω as *transfero*. In this combination μετά has the sense of an interval, a between, an across, and is thus accurately translated by the Latin *trans-*, while the Greek φέρω is, as one says, literally the same word as the Latin *fero*. Thus, μεταφέρω, to which is linked the noun μεταφορά, means to carry or bear across an interval, to transfer. But the Greek words also carry a second sense that carries these words—translates them—in another direction, a sense that disturbs the otherwise smooth transition across an interval: to transfer something is also to change it, that is—and here I am retracing a series of translations within *translation*—to alter it, and hence—this is the second sense—to pervert it. To translate or metaphorize is to bear something across an interval at the risk—perhaps even inevitably at the price—of perverting it.

In this sense the word *translation* could aptly serve to translate an exorbitant passage in Nietzsche's early, unpublished text "On Truth and Lies in a Nonmoral Sense."[3] I refer to the passage in which Nietzsche declares that the creators of language do not aim at any pure truth, at things in themselves, but rather merely express—Nietzsche uses, without marking any reservations, the word *Ausdruck*—the relations of things to humans. For such expression these creators, according to Nietzsche, lay hold of the boldest metaphors (*die kühnsten Metaphern*). Here is Nietzsche's account—in translation: "To begin with, a nerve stimulus transferred [*übertragen*] into an image! First metaphor. The image, in turn, copied [*nachgeformt*] in a sound! Second metaphor. And each time there is a complete overleaping of one sphere, right into the middle of an entirely new and different one." Thus, both images and words, both what one sees of things and what one says of them, arise by

---

similarity seems to justify this transference" (*Ad Herennium: De Ratione Dicendi*, IV.xxxiv).

3. Friedrich Nietzsche, "Über Wahrheit und Lüge in einem aussermoralischen Sinn," in vol. III 2 of *Werke: Kritische Gesamtausgabe*, ed. Giorgio Colli and Mazzino Montinari (Berlin: DeGruyter, 1973), 373.

transferal across the interval separating one sphere from another, by a transferal that is a complete overleaping from one to the other. As such the genesis of perception and of speech consists in translations that utterly pervert what gets translated. In an impossible declaration, declarable only by an operation of spacing that keeps it apart from what it declares, Nietzsche declares: "We believe that we know something about the things themselves when we speak of trees, colors, snow, and flowers; and yet we possess nothing but metaphors of things, which correspond in no way whatsoever to the original entities." But such metaphors would seem to transfer virtually nothing, to carry almost nothing from one sphere to the other. They would seem to be translations in which almost nothing—perhaps even, as Nietzsche suggests, nothing at all—gets translated. They would be bad metaphors, it seems, bad translations, so bad as almost not to be metaphors or translations at all. And we humans would seem to have—at least are declared to have—in our possession nothing but these bad translations. In place of things themselves, mistaken indeed for things themselves, at least for their truthful expression, there would be available to us humans only bad translations of these things, translations so bad as not even to be translations of the things themselves, translations that would translate next to nothing, translations that would verge on not being translations at all.

Yet, short of this extreme of abysmal perversion, translation is otherwise. Short of this limit, its alterity with respect to itself lies only in its polysemy and mobility. As in the scene in *A Midsummer Night's Dream* in which the mechanicals assemble in the woods outside Athens to rehearse the play "Pyramus and Thisbe" that they are to present at the celebration of Theseus' marriage to Hippolyta. Their director Quince the carpenter has called them together at the green plot that is to be their stage and has steered them through a most comical discussion of such problems as that of presenting on stage such fearful things as a lion (Snout the tinker exclaims: "Will not the ladies be afeard of the lion?"); and the problem of bringing moonlight into a chamber, since Pyramus and Thisbe meet by moonlight (Quince instructs: "one must come in with a bush of thorns and a lantern, and say he comes to disfigure or to present the person of Moonshine"); and the problem of presenting the wall separating Pyramus and Thisbe (Bottom the weaver declares: "Some man or other must present Wall; and let him have some plaster, or some loam, or some roughcast about him, to signify wall") (III.i.26, 55–57, 63–65). All these problems are, needless to say, problems of translation.

Just as the rehearsal begins, Puck enters and says to himself:

> What hempen homespuns have we swaggering here,
> So near the cradle of the Fairy Queen?
> What, a play toward? I'll be an auditor;
> An actor too perhaps, if I see cause.
>
> (III.i.73–76)

He is not long assuming a role at the margin of the play by which to confound it thoroughly and interrupt the rehearsal. Bottom the weaver, playing Pyramus, recites some lines and then, as Quince had instructed, exits into the brake at the edge of the green plot. As he leaves the rustic stage, reciting the promise,

> And by and by I will to thee appear,
>
> (III.i.82)

Puck declares to himself:

> A stranger Pyramus than e'er played here!
>
> (III.i.83)

Invisible to the humans, Puck follows Bottom into the brake and there does his mischief. For when Bottom steps out again on stage, the ass's head that Puck has placed on him is there for all to see, except of course for Bottom himself. Quince exclaims:

> O monstrous! O strange! We are haunted!
> Pray, masters! Fly, masters! Help!
>
> (III.i.99–100)

The mechanicals flee at the sight of Bottom with the ass's head, Snout the tinker reappearing only long enough to proclaim:

> O Bottom, thou are changed! What do I see on thee?
>
> (III.i.109–10)

Quince then also reappears momentarily, and his exclamation marks the high point of the scene. He exclaims:

> Bless thee, Bottom, bless thee! Thou art translated.
> (III.i.113–14)

Bottom's state is designated by the very same word when in the next scene Puck reports his mischievous deeds to his master Oberon, describing how he created utter confusion among the mechanicals and adding, to Oberon's enormous delight, that it was precisely upon this translated creature that Titania came to gaze when she first awoke:

> I led them on in this distracted fear,
> And left sweet Pyramus translated there;
> When in that moment, so it came to pass,
> Titania wak'd, and straightway lov'd an ass.
> (III.ii.31–34)

In this scene of translation virtually the entire range of senses of *translation* is traced—indeed not just traced but in most respects presented as in theatre, presented by way of what is presented in the play itself. Most obtrusively presented is the sense of translation as change in form, condition, appearance, or substance, translation as transformation, as transmutation into the form of an otherwise human character with an ass's head, in this case, then, translation as joining together what by nature does not belong together, translation as monstrous transformation or deformation. Yet such monsters do not exist. Humans do not in reality have the heads of asses: the scene is as in a dream or a trance. One will not readily escape being entranced as one beholds the scene; indeed one will likely be so entranced as to suspend, for instance, one's awareness of the incongruity between life-size Bottom and the tiny world of the fairies, as if Titania could, as she promises Bottom,

> . . . Purge thy mortal grossness so,
> That thou shalt like an airy spirit go.
> (III.i.153–54)

Thus transformed, thus further translated, Bottom is himself entranced, enraptured, as he is led away to the bower of the queen to be entertained by the fairies and doted on by the queen herself. Translated into the enchanting world of the fairy queen, its enchantment intensified by the effect of Cupid's flower, Bottom is doubly enraptured as,

> . . . upon this flowery bed,
>
> (IV.i.1)

he finally declares:

> I have an exposition of sleep come upon me.
>
> (IV.i.38)[4]

Here, then, is another—if archaic—sense of translation manifest in and around Bottom's—seemingly multiple—translation: translation as entrancing, enrapturing, enchanting.

The scene of Bottom's translation is prescribed in a text, a script, a scroll. As such it can be submitted to translation in the sense of reinscription in another language—as in Schlegel's German translation of the play.[5] In translating what is said into German, Schlegel cannot avoid also translating the names of the characters speaking, even though, insofar as their reference is singular and they lack meaning, proper names are, strictly speaking, untranslatable. Yet not just any proper name can be simply carried over unchanged from one language to another, especially if the name happens to coincide with or even just to suggest a common name to which a specific meaning corresponds. Little wonder, then, that the proper names in Schlegel's translation appear problematic, *Peter Quince* becoming *Peter Squenz*, the name *Robin Goodfellow* disappearing entirely in favor of *Puck*, which is translated as *Droll*, and perhaps most notably the name *Nick Bottom* being rendered as *Klaus Zettel*.

It is remarkable how Schlegel translates the exclamation that

4. Here *exposition* is a malapropism for *disposition*.

5. Shakespeare, *Ein Sommernachtstraum*, trans. August Wilhelm Schlegel, ed. Dietrich Klose (Stuttgart: Philipp Reclam, 1972).

forms the climax of the translation scene, Squenz's exclamation at the sight of Bottom's—that is, now Zettel's—translation:

> Gott behüte dich, Zettel! Gott behüte dich!
> du bist transferiert.

Here Schlegel translates Shakespeare's word into German by translating (or rather, countertranslating) the word *translated* (as in "Thou art translated") back into its Latin original *transfero.* He translates the word precisely by countertranslating it.[6]

Both as inscribed and as enacted, Quince's exclamation offers itself to translation in the sense of explicit interpretation or elucidation. Interpretation of this kind is to be distinguished from the broader, more implicit kind of interpretation that hermeneutics regards as operative in virtually all translation. One can put what Quince says into other words, explaining thus—as here—the various senses that translation can be taken to have in the exclamation. One can elucidate the complexity of meaning in the exclamation by situating it within the scene and the play as a whole. Such interpretation would allow one to show how the declaration that Bottom is translated has also a transferred or metaphorical sense,

6. On the other hand, Schlegel avoids the translation in the subsequent passage in which Puck, reporting to Oberon, says:

> I led them on in this distracted fear,
> And left sweet Pyramus translated there.
>
> (III.ii.31–32)

Schlegel's translation:

> In solcher Angst trieb ich sie weiter fort,
> Nur Schätzchen Pyramus verharret dort.

Thus, in this instance *translation,* that is, *translated,* simply goes untranslated. The avoidance is only slightly less in connection with the passage in the opening scene in which Helena, referring to Hermia, speaks of her desire

> . . . to be to you translated.
>
> (I.i.191)

Schlegel translates:

> . . . ich liess damit Euch schalten.

that is, how the figure of Bottom functions as a trope within the play as a whole. In this regard one would need to be attentive to the way in which, after the opening scene, the very fabric of the play consists in translations or nontranslations, most frequently into a dream, into the scene of a dream, so that finally, when he is relieved of the ass's head—countertranslated, one could say—Bottom speaks of nothing but the dream he has had:

> I have had a most rare vision. I have had a dream, past the wit of man to say what dream it was. Man is but an ass if he go about to expound this dream. . . . It shall be called "Bottom's Dream," because it hath no bottom.
>
> (IV.i.203–206, 214–15)

Schlegel translates the final sentence as:

> sie soll Zettels Traum heissen, weil sie so seltsam angezettelt ist.

Here one sees from a particular angle how Schlegel's translation of the name *Bottom* as *Zettel* is both peculiarly appropriate and yet limited: for, while it is no doubt the case that such a dream is only seldom instigated (*angezettelt*), its having no bottom is something quite other than the infrequency of its instigation; and while no doubt it can be said in various regards that Bottom/Zettel is an instigator, this quality is not among those alluded to in the name *Bottom*.

Whatever the connections may be through which an interpretation would contextualize and mark the metaphorical transfers operative in specific lines of the play such as Quince's exclamation that Bottom is translated, it is imperative that the interpretation take into account the fact that it has to do not just with a written text but with drama to be performed, with a text that is not primarily to be read but to be performed in the theatre. Precisely because Bottom's translation belongs to theatre, it exhibits the further sense of translation as change into another medium or sphere, as with the translation of ideas into action; but here it is a matter of the more manifold translation of a dramatic script into spectacle, action, speech, and even at certain points music.

Thus does the scene of Bottom's translation serve to present a broad range of senses of translation: as change in form, condition, appearance, or substance; as entrancing, enrapturing, enchanting; as reinscription in another language; as interpretation, elucidation; and as change into another medium or sphere. There is at least one other sense presented: translation as carrying or conveying to heaven, even (in more archaic usage) without death. It would by no means be entirely out of the question to regard what follows in the wake of Bottom's translation, his being carried off—further translated—to the bower of the fairy queen, as translating into a comedic presentation this remarkable—if archaic—sense of translation. But beyond this scene it is unmistakably broached in another, in the scene in Quince's house (IV.ii) in which the mechanicals lament that because of Bottom's disappearance and because there is no replacing him they will not be able to present their play before the duke and his company. The scene begins indeed with Starveling reporting Bottom's absence:

> He cannot be heard of. Out of doubt he is transported.
> (IV.ii.3–4)

As to another world. As from this world to the next. As prepared by the translation he underwent in the forest.[7] Thus presenting the sense of translation as conveyance to a beyond, this scene supplements the scene of Bottom's translation.

If such scenes from theatre can thus serve to present concretely the manifold senses of translation, the converse also holds: bringing certain senses of translation to bear on theatre can serve to expose the very constitution of drama. It is, in part at least, because translation figures so prominently in *A Midsummer Night's Dream* that this play is, above all, one that folds back upon itself so as to demonstrate dramatically what goes to make up drama as such. Its very title bespeaks this demonstration. For there is no more appropriate figure of drama than the dream in which images are set forth by an imagination that, as Theseus proclaims in the play,

---

7. On the debate concerning the more specific sense to be attributed to the word *transported* in this passage, see the note in the Arden edition, p. 100.

. . . gives to airy nothing
A local habitation and a name.

(V.i.16–17)

Set forth by forces that exceed what reason could ever fabricate,

. . . that apprehend
More than cool reason ever comprehends,

(V.i.5–6)

the images that haunt dreams and the theatre enchant, enrapture, entrance one who gives himself up to them, who lets himself be translated into the midst of their play. In the theatre virtually everything conspires to ensure that one dreams on, caught up ecstatically in the spell of what is said and in the shining of what appears.

Like a dream, drama has its own time. Its time is such as to suspend—while also in a sense mimicking—everyday time. Often at least it is a magical time, like that of the festival.[8] It is a time like that of midsummer night, which the Elizabethans associated with the midsummer madness brought on after days of intensive summer heat, a state characterized by a heightened receptiveness to the delusions of imagination. It is a time in which, as in the time of a dream, one lets oneself be captivated by the enchantment and magic of the scene; it is a time in which appearance is neither less nor other than being. Puck's words, addressed to the audience at the end of the play, bespeak theatre as dream and its time as the time of a dream:

If we shadows have offended,
Think but this, and all is mended,
That you have but slumber'd here
While these visions did appear.
And this weak and idle theme,
No more yielding but a dream,

8. Gadamer observes that the suspension of everyday time is a significant link of theatre to festival (Hans-Georg Gadamer, "Über die Festlichkeit des Theaters," in vol. 8 of *Gesammelte Werke* [Tübingen: Mohr Siebeck, 1993], 297–98).

Gentles, do not reprehend:
If you pardon, we will mend.

(V.i.409–16)

If the full bearing of translation on the constitution of drama is to be gauged, drama must be referred to a delimitation of the artwork as such as being in itself disclosive. Such delimitation constitutes a decisive breakthrough in that it breaks with the classical determination of the artwork as mimetic as well as with the modern redetermination of art as representation. Though by no means ventured only by what is usually called hermeneutics, such a delimitation can be sketched perhaps most economically by developing two points central to Gadamer's discussion of the artwork. (1) An artwork is not a vehicle of mimetic repetition; it does not operate by presenting in a mimetic image something other that is already there prior to, independently of, the artwork.[9] The artwork does not re-present something that would already simply have been present; it is in no sense an allegory, which would say something in order thereby to bring one to think something else. Rather than merely setting something in view again, the artwork brings to view something hitherto unseen, something even unforeseen. In this way the artwork intensifies one's vision, lets one see what one would otherwise not see. (2) And yet, in order to see that upon which the artwork opens, what is required is not that one leave the artwork behind for the sake of the vision but rather that one engage it insistently. Its opening to something unforeseen takes place in and from the work itself. The vision the artwork evokes is not a vision that passes beyond the work; rather, "one can find what it has to say only in it itself."[10] The truth of the work, its disclosive opening, is secured and sheltered precisely in the work itself. In Gadamer's hardly translatable phrase, the work achieves "die Bergung von Sinn ins Feste."[11]

9. See Gadamer's discussion of what he terms *Nachahmung* and contrasts with both the ancient and the modern determinations of mimesis (ibid., 302).

10. Gadamer, "Die Aktualität des Schönen. Kunst als Spiel, Symbol und Fest," in vol. 8 of *Gesammelte Werke*, 128.

11. Ibid., 125.

But, then, it is imperative that the work be there differently. If the disclosive opening takes place in and from the work, if, as Gadamer attests, the work is "in itself there as meaningful,"[12] then everything will hinge precisely on *how it is there*. The artwork is not simply present in the way that things of nature are present, nor even as mere artifacts or other persons are present. The artwork is there in such a way as to open disclosively as nothing else does, drawing whoever would engage it into a vision the intensity of which will never be matched by mere perception of things. How, then, is its presence so constituted that it can open upon such a vision and, in the case of the dramatic work, can draw one into the theatrical dream? The question of the dramatic work is thus one of presence, a question of the work's peculiar presence—not of presence, however, in the sense that went for so long unquestioned, not of presence as the insufficiently thought being of things, not, therefore, of presence in the sense effectively deconstructed through the work of Heidegger and Derrida, but rather another sense that deconstruction will have served precisely to free.

The presence of the dramatic work is at the same time a production of presence. This is what is distinctive about presence in the theatre: the work is present in and as a production of presence. The presence thus produced is no sheer selfsame positivity to which one would simply have added a genesis (as in describing a τέχνη). In the theatre nothing is present in the way in which something simply made (a mere artifact) is present once it has been released from the process of fabrication. Rather, the presence produced in and as theatre is more like that of the living present, which requires for its very upsurge a complicity with an immediate past that is radically not present. As time is constituted across this difference, so is the dramatic work constituted across the differences at play in it. Specifically, the dramatic production of presence takes place as a variety of translations across these fields of difference. What gives coherence to this variety is the broad sense of translation as transition across some kind of interval.

Theatre abounds in translation. There is translation, first of all,

12. Gadamer, "Dichtung und Mimesis," in vol. 5 of *Gesammelte Werke*, 85.

within language, within what is called *a* language, intralingual translation, in Jakobson's terminology. Such translation occurs not only in the metaphorical transfer of sense, in metaphorical expressions as such, but also in the transitions between one's own language and the language of an author such as Shakespeare. Translation across the difference separating the language of Elizabethan England from the English of today (in which various kinds of differentiations—and not only of dialects—continue to operate) must be carried out even simply in reading Shakespeare's text, and all the more so in entering into a performance of one of his works, either as actor or as spectator.

As soon as there is performance, another translation will have come into play, a translation of the language of the text, not into another language, but into the scenes of the play and the action carried out on those scenes. Thus enacted, the language of the written play is translated into a spectacle of action, and the translation would be across the very difference between word and deed (λόγος and ἔργον), were the deeds not themselves actions only within the theatrical dream. And yet, the drama is not merely this spectacle of deeds but rather words and deeds together. But, in turn, this conjunction is made possible by still another translation, that of the written text of the play into living, sounding speech.

Furthermore, the dramatic presentation as a whole, that is, as unity of speech, action, and scene, is carried out precisely as translation. The actors must translate themselves into the characters, without of course actually becoming those characters, producing a presence that belongs to the play but that is not their own, yet producing it precisely by means of their own presence. None of the characters depicted in *A Midsummer Night's Dream* are actually present there on stage, none even exist as such and most have never existed; yet by way of the presentation and the translation operative in it, by way of the visions thus engaged, it comes about that, in the words of Quintilian, "things absent are presented . . . in such a way that they seem actually to be before our very eyes."[13]

---

13. Quintilian, *Institutio Oratoria* VI.ii.29–30. In this passage Quintilian is referring to the rhetorical use of phantasies (φαντασίαι) or visions (*visiones*), especially in gaining power over the moods of the audience. Yet, if the phantastical

Yet, however vivid the seeming, the spectators too must translate themselves, or, more likely, let themselves be translated. They must be moved from a state in which they merely perceive the stage and those appearing upon it *to* a disposition in which they behold those persons imaginatively as the characters enacted and regard what is seen on stage as the scene of action of those characters. The spectators must give themselves over, must let themselves be entranced, enraptured, enchanted by the presence produced before their very eyes.

In the theatre nothing that one beholds is actually present as such. In the theatre one beholds only phantoms, and even whatever truth might be accorded to the words they speak is utterly compromised by their being the words of phantoms about phantoms, by their being words addressed to a scene where the presence of what seems to be is only a presence produced by and different from what actually is. Within the orbit in which being is nothing other than presence and truth is the presentation of being, theatre cannot but be declared remote from truth; it is for this reason that it has, since the ancients, never ceased to provoke suspicion. And yet, to everything one beholds in the theatre there belongs a presence the intensity of which is rarely, if ever, matched in the everyday perception of things and persons; and the intensity of this presence is only amplified by all that one hears, by the words of phantoms speaking to phantoms. The differentiation could not be more pronounced: on the one hand, the presence of what actually is, that is, the presence that is nothing other than being; on the other hand, the presence that is always other than being, the presence produced in the theatre. The very texture of this theatrical presence is translation. In its production everything is borne across a space of difference. All that makes up theatre—words, actors, spectators, etc.—all are carried away across various spaces of difference, along various itineraries of translation.

Such translations are inseparable from the force of imagination,

---

visions are taken to be such as can also be presented from the dramatic stage, what he says applies no less to the theatre.

the force that draws across intervals of difference, the force that is the very drawing by which something or someone is borne across such a space. As the spectator's vision, for instance, must be drawn beyond the persons and things actually present on stage to the phantastical scene being presented. If this tractive operation is itself pictured as the spectator's seeing through the one to the other, then this figure will have begun to communicate with one of the oldest and most decisive determinations of what comes to be translated as *imagination*; the figure will be no less than an inversion of what the Platonic texts call εἰκασία.[14]

But how is the operation of translation played out concretely in the play? As *A Midsummer Night's Dream* folds back upon itself, how does it indeed show in its own fabric the constitutive operation of translation? It does so, above all, by playing out certain kinds of translation and of nontranslation, by playing between these in the mode of comedy, or, more specifically, in that mode of comedy in which (as often in the Platonic dialogues) the very obliviousness to something serves, as it is played out, to let what has remained out of account be disclosed all the more forcefully.

Again, then, attention needs to be focused on the play within the play, not only because comedy reaches here its highest pitch but also because it is precisely with this turn that the play most openly folds back disclosively upon itself. Yet the play "Pyramus and Thisbe," which the mechanicals finally perform before Theseus and his company, is first performed in part, or rather, is rehearsed, in the scene in which Quince and his troupe assemble in the woods outside Athens. This is the scene of Bottom's translation.

But what is decisive is that, with the exception of Bottom's very special translation, there is in the case of the mechanicals almost no translation. Each of them *is* who he is, even when he is supposed to be playing some character—to be translated into a character—in the play "Pyramus and Thisbe." This simplicity is what renders so comical—indeed farcical—both their performance

14. See *Force of Imagination: The Sense of the Elemental* (Bloomington: Indiana University Press, 2000), 46–52.

of the play and their discussion, just before the rehearsal, of just how it should be performed. Their simple identity is indicated even by their names, by the fact that their names say exactly who they are, say their trades. For—with the exception of their performance of "Pyramus and Thisbe"—they are men who have never done anything but their trades—

> Hard-handed men that work in Athens here,
> Which never labour'd in their minds till now.
> (V.i.72–73)

Thus Bottom the weaver has his name from an object on which yarn is wound. Quince the carpenter is named after quines, blocks of wood used for building. The name of Snug the joiner means: close-fitting. The name of Flute the bellows mender refers to the fluted bellows used for church organs. The name of Snout, who is a tinker, that is, a mender of household utensils, refers to the spout of a kettle. And the name of Starveling the tailor bespeaks the proverbial thinness of tailors.[15]

In their simple self-identity, the mechanicals show virtually no understanding of the translation operative in theatre. Bound by their respective trades, embodying in themselves the limits definitive of each τέχνη and of τέχνη as such, each of them is bound to himself. Being who they are and nothing more or other, they cannot imagine being translated into something other, much less carry out such a translation by means of imagination. It is this entirely unimaginative, nontranslational outlook that is expressed when in the woods outside Athens they discuss the play they are about to rehearse.[16] What the discussion reveals is their obliviousness to the translations that actors and spectators must undergo in theatrical presentation.

On the one hand, they fear that the audience will take what is seen as actually present rather than as presenting a vision to be apprehended imaginatively, to be translated into a scene of the

---

15. See *The Complete Signet Classic Shakespeare*, ed. Sylvan Barnet (New York: Harcourt, Brace, Jovanovich, 1963), 533 n.

16. See R. W. Dent, "Imagination in *A Midsummer Night's Dream*," *Shakespeare Quarterly* 15 (1964): 126.

drama. They worry that Theseus and his company will regard what appears on stage simply as it is, simply as present rather than as the vehicle for a production of presence. Thus, they set about devising ways to prevent this from happening. Bottom initiates the discussion:

> There are things in this comedy of Pyramus and Thisbe that will never please. First, Pyramus must draw a sword to kill himself; which the ladies cannot abide. How answer you that?
> (III.i.8–11)

Starveling is ready to leave the killing out. But Bottom, who is to play the role, proposes instead that Quince write a prologue in which he can explain that Pyramus is not really killed and, even better, as Bottom says,

> tell them that I, Pyramus, am not Pyramus, but Bottom the weaver. This will put them out of fear.
> (III.i.19–21)

Bottom would thus have the audience told that he, Bottom, is Bottom and no one else, that he, Bottom, is not Pyramus. Such a declaration, delivered in a prologue, would in advance reestablish Bottom's simple self-identity and cancel his translation into suicidal Pyramus.

Snout, Starveling, and Bottom agree, too, that the ladies will be

> . . . afeard of the lion.
> (III.i.27)

Snout suggests another prologue. But Bottom retorts:

> Nay, you must name his name, and half his face must be seen through the lion's neck. . . . and there, indeed, let him name his name, and tell them plainly he is Snug the joiner.
> (III.i.35–36, 43–44)

Bottom's proposal is thus that Snug do as he, Bottom, will do, that he declare plainly and also show that he, Snug the joiner, is Snug the joiner and not a lion; thus, too, would he reassert his simple self-identity and retract his translation into a fearful lion.

But then, on the other hand, the mechanicals are concerned that the audience will not be able to imagine anything that is not actually seen as such on stage. For being simply themselves, they suppose the same condition to hold for what is presented on the theatrical stage: that whatever is presented must be actually present as such on stage. Thus, noting that Pyramus and Thisbe meet by moonlight, they consider how moonlight can be brought into the chamber where they will perform. They consult a calendar and confirm that the moon does shine that night; and then Bottom proposes:

> Why, then may you leave a casement of the great chamber window, where we play, open; and the moon may shine in at the casement.
>
> (III.i.52–54)

Thus would moonlight be presented by being let in through the window so as to be actually present as such there where the play is to be performed. But moonlight could be presented otherwise; it could be presented without being actually present as such. It could be presented by way of something else on the basis of which one could envisage moonlight without its actually being present as such. Such a presentation is what Quince proceeds to propose:

> Ay; or else one must come in with a bush of thorns and a lantern, and say he comes to disfigure or to present the person of Moonshine.
>
> (III.i.55–57)

It is not merely fortuitous that Quince, though a carpenter, plays the role of playwright or at least of editor and director of the play within the play. For what he proposes at this juncture could not be more decisively different from what Bottom, being who he is, has proposed. Instead of arranging for moonlight to be actually present as such on stage, Quince proposes that it be figured or presented by bringing on stage a lantern carried by a man bearing also the proverbial attribute of the man in the moon. Moonlight is to be presented without being actually present as such; it is to be presented by way of something else the presence of which is capable of transporting those with imaginative powers to a vision of moonlight. Quince's malapropism—his substitution of *disfigure* for *figure*—is not without its appropriateness: for one who, like the mechanicals, is bound to actual presence as such, all presentation will amount to a disfiguring. Even Quince, doubling as carpenter and playwright, remains to some degree bound: for even as he proposes that someone come in to present Moonshine, he declares also that this figure is to

> . . . *say* he comes to disfigure or to present the person of Moonshine.
>
> (III.i.56–57 [italics added])

He is to explain to the audience that he comes to present Moonshine, as if his mere appearance would otherwise be taken simply as what it is, as if his mere appearance could not in and of itself evoke an imaginative vision of Moonshine.

In this play Pyramus and Thisbe are to talk through the chink of a wall. The same concern that arose about the moonlight arises also about the wall. Snout says:

> You can never bring in a wall. What say you, Bottom?
>
> (III.i.61–62)

What Bottom says betrays who he is, in the double sense of the word: it is inconsistent with his being who he is, that is, amounts to his going astray from simply being who he is; and yet, it reveals who he is, who he will prove to be, namely, one who can, in the most remarkable ways, be translated. Here is what Bottom says:

> Some man or other must present Wall; and let him have
> some plaster, or some loam, or some roughcast about him,
> to signify wall; and let him hold his fingers thus, and
> through that cranny shall Pyramus and Thisbe whisper.
>
> (III.i.63–67)

Wall need not be actually present as such; like moonshine, wall can be presented by someone. Bottom explains how this presentation is to operate: the one who is to present wall is to be adorned in such a way as to *signify* wall. Here *signify* has the sense: offer some sensibly manifest indication of that which is to be signified.

Or, more to the point, it means: offer to vision some sensible content on the basis of which it can be imaginatively translated to a vision of that which is to be signified. It is perhaps a mark of Bottom's secret affinity to translation that he identifies this signifying that is at the heart of theatrical presentation and that, having identified it as the way by which someone may present wall, he—thus surpassing even Quince—forgoes prescribing that the one who comes to present wall must *say* he has come to present wall. Here, at the threshold of his own remarkable translation, Bottom broaches translation as it takes place in the theatre.

In the actual performance of "Pyramus and Thisbe" it is otherwise, and the resulting incongruity contributes a great deal to the comedic, not to say farcical, character of the play within the play. To be sure, the performance incorporates those who, as the rehearsal discussion found necessary, are to present moonshine and wall; and though indeed there is also added, as was prescribed, a prologue, the prologue completely forgoes telling what it was to have told, that Bottom is not Pyramus but Bottom the weaver. For by the time of the performance Bottom has been translated into all manner of guises other than that of Bottom the weaver.

These additions made to the play are made at considerable price: in order to include presentations of moonshine and wall as well as the Prologue, the play has to be skewed, the roles shifting such that half the actors are transposed into roles other than those initially assigned. Quince, who was to have played Thisbe's father, devotes himself instead to delivering the Prologue. Starveling, initially cast as Thisbe's mother, ends up presenting moonshine. And Snout, initially assigned the role of Pyramus' father, is transposed into the signifier of wall. These translations displace entirely the three parents, who do not appear at all in the actual performance.

With Quince, as he delivers the Prologue, it is otherwise than in what Bottom says—and, especially, does *not* say—about signifying wall. For Quince follows his artisanal compulsion to identify the signifiers, if only indexically and not by name. He says:

> This man, with lime and rough-cast, doth present
> Wall. . . .
>
> (V.i.130–31)

And then a few lines later:

> This man, with lantern, dog, and bush of thorn,
> Presenteth Moonshine. . . .
>
> (V.i.134–35)

As if these words did not suffice, both persons who come forth as signifiers also identify themselves as such. Snout identifies himself by name:

> In this same interlude it doth befall
> That I, one Snout by name, present a wall.
>
> (V.i.154–55)

Starveling's self-identification by way of the personal pronoun is only slightly more discreet:

> All that I have to say is, to tell you that the lantern is the moon; I the Man i' th' Moon; this thorn-bush my thorn-bush; and this dog my dog.
>
> (V.i.247–49)

On the other hand, no character is more insistent than Snug in identifying himself as signifier in order effectively to interrupt the frightful signifying that might otherwise be carried out:

> You ladies, you whose gentle hearts do fear
> The smallest monstrous mouse that creeps on floor,
> May now, perchance, both quake and tremble here,
> When lion rough in wildest rage doth roar.
> Then know that I as Snug the joiner am
> A lion fell, nor else no lion's dam.
>
> (V.i.214–19)

Thus would Snug, reasserting that he is who he is, forestall translation.

What, then, is played out in the rehearsal and performance of "Pyramus and Thisbe" and what is disclosed thereby? In their simple self-identity the mechanicals carry on a discourse about the theatre that is governed by their tacit allegiance to undivided presence and its corollary, the difficulty in distinguishing between theatrical presentation and simple presence as such. On the one hand, they believe that if something is presented on stage, it will be taken to be actually present as such—as with the killing and the lion. On the other hand, they believe that in order for something to be presented, it must be actually present—as with the moonlight shining in through the casement. And yet, what occurs in the course of the play is not simply an enunciation and enactment of this view; rather, in and around the enunciation and enactment of it, there is played out an *exceeding* of it. The opening of the rehearsal scene already broaches such a move, Quince presenting the place in the forest *as* a theatre, hinting at a theatrical presentation of the theatre itself:

> Pat, pat; and here's a marvelous convenient place for our rehearsal. This green plot shall be our stage, this hawthorn-brake our tiring-house; and we will do it in action, as we will do it before the Duke.
>
> (III.i.2–5)

Here already "this green plot" is translated into "our stage" and "this hawthorn-brake" into "our tiring-house" (that is, dressing room). The green plot is not simply what it is; its simple presence as such is already breached by the translation. As soon as the green plot is a stage and the hawthorn-brake is a dressing room, there is violation of simple identity and of undivided presence, as well as a retracting of that identification of presentation with presence that is the presupposition for the entire discussion that is about to commence. Within this discussion itself there is continual exceeding of this presupposition: even to foresee and hence fear that the ladies in Theseus' company might fail to distinguish the presentation of a lion from its actual presence requires that in a sense they translate themselves into their audience-to-be and into the future in which the performance will be held. But what is most striking is the way in which the exceeding of undivided presence is played out in the transition—broached by Quince—to the presenting, figuring (or disfiguring), signifying of moonshine and of wall; and, above all, when the one most susceptible to translation releases the signifier from the need to attest verbally that it is such.

In all these respects what is played out is the way in which, in and around the simple presence to which the mechanicals would adhere, differences break out and across these differences translations occur. By the way these are played out in the play, by being allowed to reopen on the ground of the mechanicals' very obliviousness to them, these differences and these translations are dramatically—indeed comically—disclosed in a more forceful and wondrous way than one could perhaps ever have imagined.

Three *Translation and the Force of Words*

Suppose, now, one were to resist the word's polysemy and mobility, which appear in theatre to be given full rein. Suppose, now, one were to take a certain distance from the tangle of senses and from the entangling, enrapturing dream of the theatre. Suppose, now, one were to restrict the word *translation* to a single meaning, to the single meaning that, currently at least, it would most readily be taken to have. Suppose, now, within a certain discursive interval, one were to translate *translation* only as transposition from one language to another—even while leaving aside the question of limits, of the limit to which resistance to the word's polysemy and mobility can be sustained, of the limit to which distancing from its multiplicity and slippage is possible, of the limit to which restriction of the word to this simple meaning can be effectively maintained.

It is to translation in this sense that Jakobson awards the designation *translation proper*. In order to distinguish other senses from this proper sense, Jakobson resorts to translating *translation*, though doing so in what would—by his own designations—have to be regarded as an improper sense. Thus he improperly translates the improper senses of *translation*, rewording *intralingual translation* as *rewording* and *intersemiotic translation* as *transmutation*, thus setting off the would-be proper sense of *translation* precisely by putting in play an improper sense. To be sure, Jakobson stops short of making the determination of the proper dependent on this operation of the improper on itself, though the independence of the proper would, it seems, have finally to be based on rigorous differentiation between intralingual and interlingual. If the singularity of languages were to be compromised, if translating within a language could be, at the same time, a translating between languages, then the sense and delimitation of proper translation would to that extent become problematic.

There are other entanglements, too, other kinds of complications that will be difficult to hold at bay indefinitely but that need to be left aside at least for a time. One of these has to do precisely with the singularity of languages, with the difficulties that arise as soon as one undertakes to specify what constitutes a single, proper language (and, hence, translation between two such languages, translation proper, in Jakobson's designation). Even if one brackets all historical, developmental considerations and maintains a strictly synchronic point of view, the fact remains that languages typically include certain foreign words and phrases that function *as* foreign elements *precisely as* they function within the language itself. In some cases they are explicitly treated as foreign additions, as when they are printed in italics. In other cases, especially in speech, the mark of their foreignness may be more subtle, and in instances where, from a diachronic point of view, a process of assimilation could be traced, it may be almost entirely effaced. Yet in every case the foreign word or phrase functions as if it belonged to two different languages; that is, from the point of view of the would-be singular language, such words and phrases function as if they both belonged and did not belong to the language. The operation of such words and phrases within a language has an effect on the limit that otherwise would determine the language in its singularity: it is as if the limit that would encircle the would-be singular language had split into two concentric circles outlining a parergonal band of undecidability. If the functioning of such words and phrases is amplified in the direction of a polylingual text—one thinks of *Finnegans Wake*[1]—then severe complications confront translation. How is one to translate a text that is written in more than one language or at least in what is not a singularly determinable language? There are also cases in which, as with Presocratic texts, an interpretation may be offered precisely as an extended translation of the text or at least as serving only to prepare the translation. How is one, then, to translate such translations?

The singularity of languages is also complicated by the way in

1. See Jacques Derrida's discussion in "Des Tours de Babel," in *Psyché*, 207–208.

which proper names function. It is not uncommon for a proper name to belong in common to more than one language, though proper names are not, on the other hand, simply indifferent to the alterity and diversity of languages. Most notorious are the complications that arise from the fact that proper names as such do not signify a meaning but rather name something singular (even where there is a certain multiplication of the singulars). To the extent that the very concept of translation is linked to the signification of meaning, it remains problematic whether and in what sense proper names can be translated. Yet translations there are. As when, in Schlegel's translation of Shakespeare's play, *Peter Quince* becomes *Peter Squenz*, *Robin Starveling* becomes *Matz Schlucker*, *Nick Bottom* becomes *Klaus Zettel*, and *Robin Goodfellow*, untranslated, is omitted altogether. Translations there are, not only such instances as these, which can hardly fail to raise questions about translation of proper names, but also instances in which the translations are thoroughly established and taken for granted, as when *Peter* becomes *Pierre*, *Elizabeth* becomes *Elsebet*, *John* becomes *Jean* or *Johann*, and *Richard* remains untranslated or, rather, remains the same in translation.

Still another complication is broached by the series of connections outlined by Aristotle in a passage that was to prove decisive for the way in which language came subsequently to be taken up as a philosophical problem. The passage is from *On Interpretation*, though it is also in a sense detached by Aristotle from this text. In translation it reads: "Spoken words are symbols of affections in the soul, and written words are symbols of spoken words. As writing is not the same for all men, so likewise speech is not the same for all. But the affections of the soul, of which these words are primary signs, are themselves the same for all, as are also the things of which these affections are likenesses."[2]

It should be noted that it is the translation that interposes the word *word* in all its occurrences in this translation. In the Greek text there occurs no word for *word* but only, in the one instance, *writing*, *inscription* (γράματα) and *the written* or *drawn* (that which has been written or drawn: γραφόμενα). In the other instance

2. Aristotle, *On Interpretation* 16a.

what is designated is *that which is in the voice* (τὰ ἐν τῇ φωνῇ). It is neither an accident nor a shortcoming that Aristotle speaks of speech as in—and, hence, as coming forth from and as—the voice. The operation of the word φωνή in speech about speech is found likewise in the Platonic texts, one of which will be examined below. It is found even in such contexts as that of the *Cratylus*, where other words that one could take as words for *word* are also operative.[3] The chief candidate is ὄνομα, which, however, ranges over a broad spectrum of senses. At one extreme it can mean *an expression* or *a saying*. At the other extreme its sense diverges in two different directions: on the one hand, it can mean *noun* in the grammatical sense as opposed to *verb* (ῥῆμα, which, however, also ranges over the same broad semantic field), while, on the other hand, it can mean *name*, not only just as proper name but also in the sense of the name one may have made for oneself by one's deeds, hence also *good name* or *fame*. The other most pressing candidate, the word λόγος, is such as to exceed the word *word* in such manifold ways—not only by its semantic range but also by its manifold of concurrent senses—that Aristotle's avoidance of it in the passage would have been virtually inevitable.

Strictly speaking, it is not just the word for *word* that is missing in the passage. In a sense the passage is not about words at all, at least not as they function normally in language, being connected to other words according to certain syntactical rules so as to express a coherent meaning. If one were to venture to translate the virtually untranslatable word λόγος as *discourse* and if one were also to adhere to what could then be called the ancient figure of discourse as weaving, then one could say that the Aristotelian passage is not about the weaving together of words into discourse but rather about the various folds both in and of the fabric of discourse. These folds belong to discourse no matter how it may

3. At the beginning of the *Cratylus* Hermogenes reports to Socrates, who is just joining the conversation, what his interlocutor Cratylus has been maintaining, namely, that there is a natural correctness of names (ὄνομα). Hermogenes explains that this means that a name is not merely "a piece of their own voice [φωνή] that people utter," that being merely voiced does not suffice to guarantee that something is truly the name of a thing (*Crat.* 383a).

happen to be woven. They are produced, not by weaving words together into expressions, but rather through a kind of translation. Or rather, through a series of translations: writing translates speech, speech translates the affections in the soul, and these affections translate things. Because this manifold is produced by translation—specifically, by translations that Aristotle regards as conveying the essential—each fold is a likeness or a symbol of that upon which it is folded. This multiple folding, this manifold that translation produces in and of the fabric of discourse, is the originary complication.

Yet none of the translations involved in producing the originary complication coincides with translation between languages, with translation in what Jakobson considers the proper sense. Inasmuch as the originary complication comes into play in and with the operation of a language, translation across the interval between two languages would presuppose the originary translations between writing, speech, affections, and things. In any case this originary manifold needs, for the moment at least, to be disregarded in order to focus on translation between different languages. What is needed is to resist—even in this originary direction—the mobility of *translation*, to restrict it to the sense of translation from one language to another, and thus to keep a certain distance from the originary complication.

Translation is inseparable from measure. In translation from one language to another, a measure must govern the transference that occurs across the interval separating the languages. It is in reference to this measure that a translation can be judged good or bad or even not a translation at all. What is the measure? The translation produced is supposed to be true to the original, true to the text (or speech) from which it is produced and of which it is alleged to be a translation. But what is this truth of translation? What does *truth* mean in this connection? Presumably it consists in the translation's corresponding to the original, in its being like the original. But what sense does correspondence have here? Correspondence in what respect? And how can a word, phrase, or sentence in one language be like a word, phrase, or sentence in another language?

It is to this question of the measure, the truth, of translation that the classical determination of translation responds. This classical determination is prepared in the Platonic dialogue *Critias*, the fragmentary sequel to the *Timaeus*. In the *Critias* the promise made in the *Timaeus* would be made good: now Critias would tell in detail the story he had only briefly outlined in the *Timaeus*, the story of the great and wonderful deeds of the original Athens, the Athens of 9,000 years ago, in its struggle against the expansionist designs of Atlantis. Already in the *Timaeus* Critias relates how the story has come down to him from his grandfather Critias, who was told it by his father Dropides, who, in turn, was told it by his relative and friend Solon. Solon, in his turn, had been told the story when he traveled to a foreign land, specifically, when he visited Saïs in Egypt, a city said also, like Athens, to have been founded by Athena, but by Athena under another name, the foreign name Neïth. Thus, Solon's story of Athens as it was indeed in the beginning was brought from a foreign land, from a foreign city whose founding and constitution had so much in common with Athens as to make it a kind of foreign double of Athens. It was there, in that foreign city, that the story had been preserved in writing, surviving thus the loss to which living memory is subject, especially when, as in Greece, much of the population has been repeatedly destroyed by natural calamities. But as preserved in this foreign place, the story had itself become foreign—foreign being understood by the Greeks primarily in reference to speech, the foreigner being precisely one who did not speak Greek. In other words, the story had been preserved, not in Greek, but in a foreign speech, in the speech of the foreign place where it was sheltered from destruction. Thus, in bringing the story back to Athens from this foreign place, perhaps even in order to recover the full story as such, Solon was faced with the problem of translation.

It is in the *Critias* that Critias describes how Solon dealt with this problem. The passage on Solon's translation occurs, most appropriately, at that point in the dialogue where, having spoken of ancient Athens, Critias is about to tell of Atlantis; in the narrative, as in translation as such, it is a matter of transition between one's own and the foreign. It is precisely to forestall a certain confusion regarding these that Critias interrupts the narrative and speaks briefly of translation.

Here—in (my own) translation—is how he begins: "Briefly, before the account [λόγος], it is necessary to explain something, lest perhaps you wonder at hearing Greek names of foreign men ['Ελληνικὰ βαρβάρων ἀνδρῶν ὀνόματα]. The cause of these you will now learn."[4]

What the explanation is to forestall is the wonder or astonishment that might be provoked by hearing names that, though they are the names of foreigners, are Greek rather than foreign. Although, from this point on, the story is even more thoroughly foreign, not only recovered from a foreign place but largely about still another foreign place, Critias is to narrate it in Greek, saying even the names of foreign men (the rulers of Atlantis) entirely in Greek. Or rather, *almost* entirely in Greek: for there is one notable exception near the beginning of Critias' account of Atlantis. The account begins by referring again, as at the beginning of the account of ancient Athens, to the gods' portioning out of the whole of the earth. Critias relates that Poseidon took for his allotment the island of Atlantis. Not only did he form and shape the island, surrounding the acropolis with circular belts of sea and land enclosing one another alternately, but also he begat of a mortal woman, Cleito (daughter of one originally sprung from the earth itself), five pairs of twin sons. Having then divided the island of Atlantis into ten portions, Poseidon set about assigning to each son two things: first, a portion of the island over which to rule, and, second, a name (ὄνομα). The firstborn of the eldest twins was assigned the acropolis and its surroundings, and there he was to reign as king over the others; his name, as Critias states it, was thoroughly Greek. And yet, from Critias' earlier explanation one knows that the name of the king almost certainly cannot have been (as Critias says) Atlas; it must, rather, have been a foreign name, which subsequently came to be translated as Atlas. But then the island and the ocean, which share his name, cannot have had the names At-

4. Plato, *Critias* 113a.

lantis and Atlantic but must have had—from Poseidon—other, foreign names. One realizes that the names Critias is using in his account—names that will have resulted from translation—replace the original, foreign names. The story of the island of Atlantis is thus in fact the story of an island that the Greeks called Atlantis but that itself almost certainly bore (natively, as it were) another, foreign name that remains unknown to—or at least unsaid by—Critias. The translational replacement of the original, foreign names has the effect of undoing the assignment of names carried out by the god himself. Hence, such translation represents, within this perspective at least, a subversive and excessive venture on the part of mortals.

Yet it is not the name of the king that is the exception but rather that of his twin brother. To this second-born of the eldest twins Poseidon assigned a portion of the island extending from an extremity near the pillars of Heracles up to the region now called Gadeira. As in every case, Poseidon assigned him also a name. But in his case, unlike the others, Critias says the name not only in Greek translation but also in its original, foreign form: his name, says Critias, was "Eumelus in Greek, but Gadeirus in the native [speech]."[5] The mention of the original, foreign name—foreign to Greeks but native to inhabitants of the island that Greeks call Atlantis—serves at the very least as a reminder that all the other names that occur in Critias' discourse about the island kingdom and its exploits are results of translation. The survival of this original, foreign name in a discourse otherwise entirely in Greek is presumably to be attributed to its consonance with the still current place name Gadeira. This particular connection serves to point up the significance that the connection between name and place has throughout the *Critias* and especially in Poseidon's assignments to his sons. In Critias' speech about their names, there occur the two words χώρα and τόπος, around which the most abysmal discourse of the *Timaeus* circles, a discourse (chorology) that ventures even beyond what will come to be called place. And when Critias says the foreign name of the son called Eumelus in Greek, the word

5. Ibid., 114b.

he uses to identify the name Gadeirus as other than Greek, as belonging to the indigenous speech of Atlantis, is simply ἐπιχώριον: native, belonging to the country, to the χώρα.

The beginning of the passage on translation is oriented primarily by the word ὄνομα: the concern (which makes an explanation necessary) is with the effect of certain names, of Greek names used for foreign men, whose names would not have been Greek but foreign. Not only does the word ὄνομα orient the passage from the beginning, orienting indeed the entire passage on translation, but also the word imparts to the entire passage its peculiar polysemy. Its most apparent sense at the beginning of the passage is that of *name*, indeed *proper name*. The concern is with the effect of the Greek names used for foreign men, as—to take the exceptional case—with the use of the Greek name Eumelus for the foreigner whose name, as both he and Poseidon would have said it, is Gadeirus. Yet as long as ὄνομα has the sense of *proper name*, translation will remain problematic, in particular the very translations that Critias goes on to consider in the passage. How can a proper name in the speech indigenous to the island that Greeks call Atlantis be translated into a Greek proper name? Perhaps only insofar as the former is more than a proper name, insofar as it also functions as a common noun that does not just name a singular but also signifies a meaning. Is it at such a transition that the Platonic text hints by ascribing to the one person whose foreign name is stated a Greek name that very transparently doubles as a common noun? As if the Greek name Εὔμηλος, which means *rich in sheep*, could have been arrived at via this meaning. As if Γάδειρον might have had some such meaning and thus have been appropriately translated by Εὔμηλος.

But then once ὄνομα assumes the sense of *common noun*, the expressed concern shifts. What now might prompt wonder are, for instance, the various words by which, in Greek, foreign men might be characterized—that certain ones are heroes or statesmen or philosophers. But then the sense of ὄνομα will easily extend to whatever is said, in Greek, of foreign men, assuming thus the broad sense of *an expression* or *a saying*, approximating (at least in this dimension) to the sense of λόγος, the word used by Critias to designate the entire discourse on Atlantis, easily extended, in turn, to Critias' entire discourse as such. The slippage of the word ὄνομα would thus serve to broaden the passage on the translation of names into a description of how the entire story narrated by Critias came to be translated.

Critias continues with a sentence that may be translated as follows: "As Solon was planning to make use of the story [λόγος] in his own poetry, he found, on investigating [διαπυνθανόμενος] the force of the names [τὴν τῶν ὀνομάτων δύναμιν], that those Egyptians who had first written them down had translated them into their own voice [εἰς τὴν αὑτῶν φωνὴν μετενηνοχότας]."

In reporting that Solon was planning to make use of the story in his own poetry, Critias is reiterating what he said in the *Timaeus*. In the earlier report Critias indicated that Solon did not in fact succeed in carrying out his plan. Critias cites two reasons: first, Solon pursued his poetry only as something ancillary (πάρεργον), and, second, he was compelled to put it aside on account of the evils in Athens with which he had to contend upon his return from Egypt. Critias is of the opinion that if it had been otherwise, if Solon had been able to carry out his plan of rendering the story in Greek poetry, "then neither Hesiod nor Homer nor any other poet would ever have proved more famous than he."[6] In a word, he would have made a name for himself as a poet.

In order to have rendered the story in Greek poetry, he would have had to translate the writings in which it had been recorded, the writings that he was shown while in Egypt.[7] He would have had to translate these writings at least to the extent necessary for retelling the story in Greek; in other words, he would have had to produce a translation at least in the sense of a retelling of the story in Greek. What about the proper names of the foreigners who figure in the story, of those from the island and empire that Greeks call Atlantis? Perhaps, from considerations of prosody, Solon would

6. Plato, *Timaeus* 21c–d.

7. Critias reports that the Egyptian priest under whose tutelage Solon was taken told him briefly about the laws and the noblest of deeds performed by the ancient Athenians. Yet the priest promised that at their leisure they would go through the full story in exact order and detail, taking up the writings themselves (ibid., 23e–24a).

have preferred to translate these names into Greek. Or perhaps, lest auditors wonder at hearing Greek names of foreign men, he would have chosen to leave these names untranslated.

Yet he had no such choice. This is what he found out once he set about investigating the matter. He found that those Egyptians who had first written the names down had translated them. Hence, in the writings that Solon was shown in Egypt, the foreign names, the names foreign to both Greek and Egyptian, have already been replaced by translations. In these writings there is already reason for concern about the effect such names might have, about the astonishment that could be prompted by hearing Egyptian names of foreign men. Yet in the Egyptian writings their own names, the names they would have called themselves and would in the case of his sons at least have been called by Poseidon, are completely effaced, with, it seems, the exception of Gadeirus. Short of translating back from the Egyptian names, that is, countertranslating, there is no means of retrieving their original names, the names native to them but foreign to Greek and Egyptian. The loss of their names is hardly less definitive than that of Atlantis itself, which "sank into the sea and vanished,"[8] leaving no trace of itself except the shoal that made the ocean at that spot impassable, just as there was left from the original names only the traces provided by their Egyptian translations.

But what is the sense of translation here and how does it take place? Critias says that the Egyptians translated the names into their own voice (φωνή). Or, if one translates *translation* back, as it were, into Greek: they carried them over, transferred them (the word is a form of μεταφέρω) into their own voice. Here, too, as in Aristotle and in other Platonic texts, what one might otherwise call speech is spoken of as the voice, as taking place in and as the voice, as phonation. In translating, the Egyptians carried the foreign names over into their own voice. Having done so, or as a way of effecting the transfer, they wrote down the names.

But how did Solon, as Critias says, discover that the Egyptians who had first written down the names had translated them

8. Ibid., 25d.

into their own voice? Critias attests that Solon did so by investigating, by carrying out a thorough search through questioning (διαπυνθάνομαι). Nothing dictates of course against assuming that Solon may have addressed questions to certain Egyptians he met in Saïs, for instance, to the old priest under whose tutelage he was taken. Yet Critias' account states unequivocally that the object of Solon's investigation was the force of names. Whatever questions may have been addressed to the Egyptians would have been directed precisely to this goal, to searching out the force of names. He could, assuming a common speech, have asked someone about the status of the names. He could have asked the old priest, for instance, about the voice in which the names of the various leaders of the now-sunken island were inscribed. He could have asked the old priest whether these names, as they had once been written down by Egyptian scribes, were Egyptian names or not, assuming that if they were not Egyptian they must have been in the voice of those who inhabited the island. Yet, even if the old priest had presumed to answer and had informed Solon that indeed all the names were Egyptian, the breach of singularity belonging to each voice forestalls all certainty in this regard. For there is nothing to prevent a name from belonging to more than one voice, most notably, but not exclusively, in the case of proper names. There is nothing to guarantee that a name inscribed in Egyptian is not also a name in the voice—now presumably extinct—indigenous to the island called (by Greeks) Atlantis. That the names by which certain leaders of the island are called in the Egyptian writings appear Egyptian—and a native speaker can presumably determine this almost unfailingly—does not establish conclusively that these names result from translation and not from repetition. Even if, merely repeated at the time of inscription, they had once seemed foreign to the Egyptian voice, the assimilation that the antiquity of the writings would have permitted would have served to efface their alterity.

One could suppose, then, that this inevitable uncertainty is what led Solon not just to ask the Egyptians about the names in the Egyptian writings but to investigate the force of these names. The force (δύναμις) of a name lies in its being capable (δύναμαι), in its being capable of accomplishing that which it is proper to a name to accomplish. What is proper to a name as such is that it announce something or someone, that it announce that which it names. In announcing what it names, the name presents it, makes it present in a certain way, in a way that philosophy—from Plato on—distinguishes from the way in which sense perception (αἴσθησις) makes things present. A name is capable, then, of making present in a certain way that which it names even when what it names is not at all present to sense perception, even when it could not be present to sense perception, even when it has passed away so as never again to be able to come before sense perception, even when it has not yet come to be so as to be able to come before sense perception, even when it is such that it could never come before sense perception. The force of a name is thus its capacity to make manifest that which it names, to draw it forth into a certain manifestness that is, in a certain way, independent of perceptual manifestness. This is why names, especially when they are preserved in writing, are the repository of memory. Just as he is about to begin his discourse in the *Critias*, a discourse in which nothing figures more prominently than names, which are themselves to be recalled in order that the Athenian beginning be remembered—as he is about to begin Critias calls upon all the gods, but most of all upon Mnemosyne, "for nearly all the most important part of our account [λόγος] depends on this goddess."[9]

In investigating the force of names, Solon would, then, have searched out—with or without assistance from the Egyptians he met in Saïs—the capacity of the names in question to make manifest that which they name. And, in investigating that force, Solon would—with or without assistance—have put the force in force, that is, would have let the names exercise their capacity to make manifest that which they name. Investigating them in their exercise of this capacity to make manifest, he would, in turn, have gained a measure of this capacity, a measure of their force. How, then, was it that by investigating the force of names Solon discovered that the names had been translated, that the names written down long ago by the Egyptian scribes were translations, not the

9. Plato, *Critias* 108d.

original, native names of those told of in the account? It can only have been by way of the measure he gained of the force of the names. It can only have been through his discovering a certain incapacity of the names in their translated form, through his finding the force of the names inscribed in the Egyptian writings to be weak, as measured, most immediately, against the force of such names as he would have said in his own voice. That those inscribed names were translations can have been attested only by their relative incapacity to make manifest that which they name, by their leaving that which they name still in some measure concealed, resistantly closed off, precisely as though it were foreign. Here one finds indicated for the first time what later—and especially in modern times—will be ever more insistently declared: that translation cannot occur without loss, that in a translation the force of names will always have been diminished, that in translation names undergo a loss of force. Again and again it will be said that a translation is always less forceful than its original.

In translating into their own voice the proper names of certain inhabitants of the island that Greeks call Atlantis, the Egyptian scribes could hardly have avoided also translating what, in the voice of those inhabitants, had been said of them. The scribes can hardly have avoided translating, for instance, the name that certain of them made for themselves, that is, the fame, the reputation, that would of course have been declared, not merely by citing proper names, but by words, common nouns and verbs, describing their qualities and their deeds. Thus, there is good reason to suspect that virtually everything the Egyptian scribes wrote down would have been a translation, that the writings Solon was shown in Egypt were nothing but translation.

In any case, since Solon's intent was to use the story for his own poetry, it was his task to translate these writings into Greek, that is, to convey them into his own voice: "So he himself, in turn, retrieved the thought [διάνοια] of each name and leading [ἄγων] it into our own voice wrote it out."

Beginning in each case with an Egyptian name, Solon's first move was to retrieve the thought of the name; then, in a second move, he led, directed, drew, this thought into his own voice, into the voice of Greeks; then, as a final move or as the consummation of the second move, he wrote down the Greek name. Here for the first time the structure, the basic constitution, of translation is determined; here the Platonic text declares what may be called the protoclassical determination of translation. But in this determination everything depends on how the single word διάνοια is understood. Very few words prominent in the Platonic texts appear, on the one hand, so readily translatable and yet are, on the other hand, so resistant to translation into all those modern words that one would attempt, as it were, to translate back into διάνοια. Following the itinerary of this word in the *Republic*, for instance, could hardly not have the effect of persuading one to leave the word literally untranslated and to translate it only in the sense of surrounding it with a discourse in which its sense could be adumbrated.[10] But even if—conceding, hesitantly and with reservations, to a certain tradition of translation—one were to translate διάνοια as *thought* or *intention* (limiting these words, as would be necessary, by reference to a well-defined philosophical sense, as in phenomenology), it remains ambiguous. For, thus translated, the word could designate either thinking or that which is thought through the thinking, either the intending or that which is intended by it. Even aside from considerations of the correlativity of the noetic and noematic sides, there is good reason to retain the ambiguity, but in the form of a duality: for Solon's task was to retrieve the thought, which he could have done only by carrying out to some degree the thinking through which the thought (that which is thought) is thought, that is, by enacting the thinking of the thought, the intending of the intended (*intentum*). Specifically, then, Solon's retrieval would have taken the form of an enactment in which he would have come to intend that which is intended through the name. But that which is intended, that which the name names, is nothing other than that which the name, through its force, can make manifest. Solon's retrieval of the διάνοια of a name would thus have taken the form of an enactment in which the force of the name would be released, would be put in force in

10. See *Being and Logos: Reading the Platonic Dialogues*, 3rd ed. (Bloomington: Indiana University Press, 1996), 424–43.

such a way that what is named would be made manifest. The retrieval of the διάνοια of a name, which would constitute the first move of translation, would already have been carried out in the investigation of the force of the name, the investigation by which Solon found out that the Egyptian text was in fact a translation. Indeed the retrieval of the διάνοια of a name would have been carried out even short of the explicit gauging of this force that is required in order to expose it as a translation.

What would not, however, have been carried out is the decisive second move that translation requires, the move in which the διάνοια would be drawn into his own voice. It is in this second move that all the complications and difficulties of translation will prove to be concentrated. For what it requires is that one discover in one's own voice a name that not only names the διάνοια—the very same διάνοια named in the other voice—but also is of such force as to be capable of making manifest that which it names, of bringing it to presence in that certain way appropriate to names. Though this second move brings one from the foreign back to one's own, it is decidedly not a matter merely of retrieval, of grasping again what has been said, but of saying what has never yet been said in one's own voice.

As the passage on translation proceeds, it shifts ever more decisively from focusing merely on proper names to consideration of discourse as such. Nothing points this up so clearly as Critias' remark immediately following the passage: "And these very writings [resulting from Solon's writing down the names in translation] were in the possession of my grandfather and are now in mine, and as a child I learned them by memory." There is every reason to believe that what was translated and written down in and as these writings handed down to Critias himself from his grandfather was the entire story as such and not merely the proper names of those who figured prominently in it.

One could conclude, then, that the passage from the *Critias* constitutes a discourse on translation as such. From it issues the inaugural determination of translation, the protoclassical determination, which subsequently comes to be stabilized by reference to the distinction that itself comes to be stabilized as fundamental to philosophy (so radically so as to determine the very sense of fundamental). Through this double stabilization the classical determination of translation is constituted. In those few instances in the history of philosophy where translation again surfaces as a question, only scant deviation from this classical determination is to be found. Even when Nietzsche declares certain would-be fundamental translations to be utter perversions of what would be translated, when he describes them as overleaping from one sphere into another without carrying anything over, as translations that translate nothing, the parameters of this discourse are still governed by the classical determination of translation precisely as this discourse overturns that determination, inverts it, and gestures, perhaps, beyond.

In the protoclassical determination that issues from the *Critias*, the force of names figures prominently. Retrieving the διάνοια of a name requires that the name not be simply and emptily repeated in the manner all too familiar from everyday speech; retrieving the διάνοια requires, rather, that the force of the name be released so that, through its force, the name comes to make manifest that which it names. Drawing the διάνοια into one's own voice requires a search within one's own voice that could be carried out only by voicing various names, not in mere repetition, but in such a way as to release and at the same time to measure their force. Only through such a search could one—if at all, for untranslatability is not ruled out—find a name that names the very same διάνοια with force sufficient to make it manifest; and only if a name has such force is it possible, by releasing the force, to confirm that the name names the very same διάνοια named in the other voice. Thus, as conveyance of the διάνοια across from one voice to another, translation is engaged with the force of names, with enactments that release and measure such forces. Indeed it is the force of names that, above all, enables translation.

In the stabilization that produces the classical determination of translation, the διάνοια is secured as νοητόν over against the αἰσθητόν. Or if, for the moment, one merely resumes what is perhaps the most decisive and questionable translation in the history of the West, the translation of the basic words of Greek philosophy into Latin, then one may say: in the classical determination the διάνοια is secured as intelligible over against the sensible character of the name.[11] With the διάνοια thus secured as intelligible being, the orientation is shifted away from the manifestation effected by the name, away from the force by which a name makes present that which it names. If what is named, that is, the διάνοια, is perpetually present as such, then the capacity of a name to let it be present has diminished significance and finally comes to be constitutively linked to merely human limitations. For a name to name something no longer entails that in some measure it makes manifest what it names, that it names it in and as making it manifest, bringing it to presence. In place of such naming as making manifest, what becomes definitive is the abstract relation between the name and the διάνοια named, which is determined as intelligible and eventually as signification or meaning. In a curious reversion to a position not unlike one of those that in the *Cratylus* was unhinged in and into comedy,[12] everything comes to depend on the abstract relation of the name to its signification or meaning. Once names thus become signifiers, the very sense of the force of names will have been lost.

The classical concept of translation thus makes no mention of the capacity of names to make manifest; in this determination all reference to the force of names has disappeared, or if a trace is still indicated, it is no more than a vestige now quite ineffective. The schema that constitutes this determination is correspondingly simple: translation consists in the movement from a unit in one language (word, phrase, sentence, etc.) to a corresponding unit in the other language, this movement being carried out by way of circulation through the signification, the meaning. Begin-

---

11. It proves necessary to repeat this securing with respect to the name itself. For a name is not just a singular sensible occurrence, not just, for instance, a singular sound or series of sounds uttered by a speaker at a certain time. A name can be repeated at various times and uttered by various speakers, and there will be considerable variation among these instances, no one of which can be identified as the name itself. This "ideality" of the name requires, then, that a distinction be drawn between the name itself, which can never be uttered or heard as such and which is thus stabilized as intelligible, *and* the various instances in which there is a sensible utterance or inscription of the name.

12. See *Being and Logos*, chap. 4.

ning with, for instance, a word in one language, one passes to the meaning in order then, from the meaning, to pass to the corresponding word in the other language. In this determination the sense of correspondence, the truth of translation, is also determined: a translation is true to its original if it has the same meaning. The measure of translation is restitution of meaning.

At least with units larger than a single word, translation will usually require syntactic as well as semantic strategies. It is well known that what is expressed by certain words in a certain syntactic structure in one language often can prove expressible in another language only through a very different syntactic structure. In some cases certain words in the one language can be conveyed in the other language, not as such, but only through certain syntactic strategies; such is often the case, for instance, with Greek particles. But whatever the syntactic transformations required, they are entirely in service to the restitution of the meaning of certain linguistic units. Even if, for instance, in translating poetry, there may be reason to preserve certain syntactical structures along with meter and rhyme, all such strategies are, in the end, to be subordinated to the ideal of saying in the translation precisely what the text—in smaller or larger segments or even just as a whole—means.

In this classical determination there is reference neither to the manifestive force of names nor to any enactment that would release and measure such force. To the extent that the Greek name for name—that is, ὄνομα—has its very sense determined by reference to manifestive force, one will be compelled to admit that none of the translations proposed for it, not even the translation *name*, to say nothing of *word*, *phrase*, *expression*, etc., are true to it, not at least insofar as all these modern names for what the Greeks called ὄνομα are governed by the classical determination of translation or at least by a determination of language as such that corresponds to it. Even the word *language* is itself something less than a true rendering of that by which one could take the Greeks to have designated the same phenomenon. It is not just that *language* would render both τὰ γραφόμενα and τὰ ἐν τῇ φωνῇ (as we say, both writing and speech), but, more significantly, that with *language* one says abstractly what the Greeks said with remarkable phenomenal concreteness: for what is called *language* comes to pass phenomenally precisely as inscription or as voice. What is called *language* occurs, happens—indeed is—only as an inscription or a voicing of names.[13]

The classical determination of translation is in force in Cicero's reflections and no doubt in his practice of translation. Its schema is clearly discernible in *The Best Kind of Orator* (*De Optimo Genere Oratorum*), a work dated 46 B.C. though not published in Cicero's lifetime. The work was to serve as an Introduction to Cicero's translations of Demosthenes' *On the Crown* and Aeschines' *Against Ctesiphon*, though these translations were never published nor perhaps ever completed. In any case they provided an occasion for Cicero to reflect on what is at stake in translation and on what his specific intentions were.

In the first of the two passages devoted to this reflection,[14] Cicero begins by referring to the two orators he has translated, characterizing them as the two most eloquent Attic orators and noting that the orations translated were speeches that Demosthenes and Aeschines delivered against each other. Cicero then indicates his specific intent, the capacity in which he went about translating these orations: "And I did not translate them as an interpreter but as an orator. . . ." Two things, he says, had to be retained: ". . . keeping the same thoughts [*sententia*] and the forms, or as one might say, the 'figures' of thought. . . ." Retention of the same thoughts or meaning is required for translation as such in its classical determination; retention of the figures of thought is secondary in that it is prescribed by the specific character of the works, that they are orations, and by Cicero's specific intent to translate them as an orator. While thus keeping the same thoughts

13. The Greek designation of speech as φωνή or as τὰ ἐν τῇ φωνῇ is not, then, just another instance in which speech as such is designated by the name of an anatomical part indispensable to its production. It is not simply an alternative to the ancient Hebrew designation of speech as lip or the Latinate and modern designation of speech as tongue, which is retained etymologically in *language*. For unlike the lip and the tongue, voice is not itself an anatomical part but rather the very guise in which speech occurs. It is only as voice, only in the sounding of a voice, only in the voicing of names, that speech occurs and so is.

14. Cicero, *De Optimo Genere Oratorum* V.14 and VII.23.

and figures, he does so, as he adds, ". . . in words that conform to our usage." The schema of the classical determination, supplemented by the oratorical specificity, is clearly in place: the translation consists primarily in saying in Latin words the same thoughts as were said in the Greek words of the orators.

The second passage reiterates and extends what is said in the first. Cicero refers to the virtues of the speeches he has translated and expresses his hope that the translation retains these virtues. Three virtues are named: first, the thoughts; second, the figures of thought; and third (extending the oratorical specificity), the order of topics. He says that, while retaining these three virtues of the original, he has proceeded by "following the words only insofar as they are not abhorrent [*non abhorreant*] to our usage." His point is, on the one hand, the same as in the first passage: translation is a matter of carrying the three virtues over into words belonging to the native way of speaking. But, on the other hand, it is also a matter of determining just which words to translate as such and how exactly to translate them, of determining these specifics of the translation by reference to usage, to what is "not abhorrent to our usage." Thus Cicero goes on to say specifically: "if all the words are not directly translated from the Greek, we have at least tried to keep them within the same kind [*genus*]." This reference to specific translational strategies that would diverge from direct transfer (from one word to an exact equivalent) is amplified in the first passage, which concludes: "And in so doing, I did not hold it necessary to render [*reddere*] word for word [*verbum pro verbo*], but I preserved the general kind and force of the words [*sed genus omne verborum vimque servavi*]. For I did not think I ought to count them out to the reader like coins, but to pay them by weight, as it were." A word-for-word rendering is not necessary as long as the same thoughts and figures (and perhaps order) are retained, and such retention, Cicero suggests, is possible provided one preserves the general kind and force of the words. A word-for-word rendering is not only superfluous but, he further suggests, not even very desirable (assuming that it is possible). What counts is that the words be rendered in a way that sustains, not the individual words, but the sense of what is said, the thoughts. To this end the same general kind of words need to be used in the translation, and words need to be used that retain the force that the words of the original have.

Cicero's reflection on translation thus inscribes the classical schema by which translation consists primarily in carrying the meaning of a unit in one language over to a corresponding unit in the other language. The schema does not exclude requirements specific to the text or to the intent of the translator; neither does it exclude the various strategies by which units and their limits would be shifted and syntactical structures transformed in the course of translation. Yet all these supplementary moments would continue to be rigorously linked to or governed by the requirement that the meaning of what the original says, its thoughts, be rendered in the translation. Cicero grants that one of the things needed for such restitution is that the force of the words be preserved. In the word translated as *force*, the word *vis*, Cicero's text retains a trace of the protoclassical determination. But *vis* is not δύναμις, even if it translates—yet without translating—δύναμις; it is only a trace marking the absence of what had once been thought in the Platonic discourse. With Cicero the word for force has lost the force that δύναμις once had.

The classical determination of translation is nowhere more clearly and succinctly presented than in a passage in Locke's *An Essay Concerning Human Understanding*. The passage occurs in Book III, entitled "Of Words," and is thus set within the context of Locke's general theory of language. The primary moments of this theory are expressed when Locke, noting that man was by nature fashioned so as to be capable of producing articulate sounds, observes that man could then make these sounds "stand as marks for the ideas within his own mind, whereby they might be known to others, and the thoughts of men's minds be conveyed from one to another."[15] Thus, for Locke, two connections are definitive of language: it consists of words, which, first, stand for ideas and which, second, make it possible for these ideas to be communicated from one man to another. These two functions of words, to signify

15. John Locke, *An Essay Concerning Human Understanding*, in vols. 1 and 2 of *The Works of John Locke* (London, 1823; reprint, Aalen: Scientia Verlag, 1963), Book III, chap. i, §2 (in this edition Book III is found in vol. 2).

and to communicate, are intimately linked: because the ideas that words signify are invisible, internal, they could not be communicated otherwise than by means of the signifying words. Since society requires communication, "it was necessary that man should find out some external sensible signs, whereof those invisible ideas, which his thoughts are made up of, might be made known to others." Thus it was that words came "to be made use of by men, as the signs of their ideas."[16]

What words announce are thus neither the things nor the meanings (in the Greek sense, as νοητόν) spoken of but rather the invisible ideas interior to our minds. Locke insists on this connection, on its exclusivity, even suspending for its sake the question of representation: "words in their primary or immediate signification stand for nothing but the ideas in the mind of him that uses them, how imperfectly soever or carelessly those ideas are collected from the things which they are supposed to represent."[17] Indeed Locke goes so far as to declare that to make words stand for anything but the ideas in our minds is a perversion of the use of words and a cause of obscurity and confusion.

Yet, for all his insistence, Locke privileges the names of simple ideas so as to allow that they "intimate also some real existence, from which was derived their original pattern."[18] Locke does not explain how such intimation would operate, how it not only would presumably link an idea to some real existence but also, presumably by way of the idea, would link the name of the idea to such existence.[19] Instead, he goes on to develop the thesis that the names of simple ideas are not capable of any definition. By a definition he means: "the showing the meaning of one word by several other

16. Ibid., III.ii.1.

17. Ibid., III.ii.2.

18. Ibid., III.iv.2.

19. Locke himself acknowledges in the *Essay* the difficulty of establishing any connection between ideas and the reality of things. In its most succinct form: if the mind perceives nothing but its own ideas, how is it to know that these ideas agree with things themselves? In the case of simple ideas he attempts to address this difficulty by having recourse to nature, to the naturalness of the way in which things operate on the mind to produce simple ideas. See my discussion in *Force of Imagination*, 86–87.

not synonymous terms."[20] Yet *meaning*, for Locke, is synonymous with *idea*, so that to show the meaning of a word is to elicit by other words the idea signified by the word. To give a definition of a word is, then, to offer a series of words not synonymous with it that are capable of eliciting the very idea that the word stands for. Hence, Locke's demonstration that the names of simple ideas are incapable of being defined: "the several terms of a definition, signifying several ideas, they can all together by no means represent an idea, which has no composition at all: and therefore a definition, which is properly nothing but the showing the meaning of one word by several others not signifying each the same thing, can in the names of simple ideas have no place."[21] Since a definition must consist of several words, each signifying an idea, a definition can signify only a composite of the several ideas, not an incomposite, simple idea. Locke seems to have no doubts about the one-to-one correlation assumed to hold between word and idea; one wonders whether his confidence might have been disturbed by, for instance, the definition of shape (σχῆμα) that Socrates offer in the *Meno*, that (in translation) "shape is the only thing found always following color."[22]

Locke's confidence would seem, on the other hand, to be bolstered by the examples that he goes on to mention, examples intended to demonstrate the futility of attempting to give definitions of simple ideas. It is precisely in this context that he comes to refer to translation. In his first example only the word is lacking: he supposes a situation in which a Dutchman is asked what *beweeginge* means—that is, one may say, a situation in which the Dutchman is asked to define *beweeginge*, a definition that cannot but be a translation, indeed even if it should fail to be a proper definition. The translation—one will note how questionable it is, especially if one recalls the Greek original—might be in English: " 'The act of a being in power, as far forth as in power.' " Or it might be in Latin: " '*actus entis in potentia quatenus in potentia*.' "[23] Locke has only scorn

20. Locke, *Essay*, III.iv.6.

21. Ibid., III.iv.7.

22. Plato, *Meno* 75b.

23. Locke, *Essay*, III.iv.8.

for such alleged definitions, such "exquisite jargon." Suppose that someone were to receive such a definition: "I ask whether any one can imagine he could thereby have understood what the word 'beweeginge' signified, or have guessed what idea a Dutchman ordinarily had in his mind, and would signify to another, when he used that sound."[24] These cannot, in Locke's terms, be definitions of this name of a simple idea, of the name *beweeginge*, though they are translations, even if bad ones.

The most significant passage concerning translation occurs as Locke turns to another example in which alleged definitions prove to be, not definitions at all, but only translations. He refers to the atomists' alleged definition of motion as a passage from one place to another. Here the problem is that one word (*passage*) replaces another (*motion*) with which it is synonymous, with which it shares the same meaning. In the alleged definition of motion, what occurs is motion from one word to another with the same meaning, that is, circulation from one to the other by way of the common meaning. Thus Locke declares: "This is to translate, and not to define, when we change two words of the same signification one for another."[25] One notices that Locke does not restrict translation to transferal between different languages: whether one substitutes for *motion* the Latin *motus* or the English *passage*, it remains a matter simply of translation. In both cases it is a matter of movement across a difference, either within a language or between languages; in this movement from one word to another, the meaning—for Locke, the idea—is both what is carried over and what makes the movement as such possible.

Locke thus reiterates quite precisely the classical determination of translation as transition or transfer from one word to another by way of circulation through the common meaning. This reiteration is especially remarkable in view of the philosophical remoteness of Locke's work from the Greek context in which this determination was forged; there is perhaps no better index of this

24. Ibid.

25. Ibid., III.iv.9.

remoteness than the difference separating what the Greeks called διάνοια—and also ἰδέα—from those internal objects of thought that Locke called ideas. What is remarkable is that the classical determination could continue to govern the concept of translation even across this enormous difference.

Gadamer's hermeneutical discussion of translation reaffirms the classical determination yet also underlines the limit, the incompleteness, of translational restitution of meaning, as well as a certain inevitable distortion produced by translation. The discussion is restricted to translation from one language to another, to translation as passage of meaning across the differential interval between two languages. The discussion is also largely strategic: it is oriented to elucidating the conditions of understanding as such, to elucidating these conditions by focusing on situations in which understanding is disrupted or made exceptionally difficult, as, for instance, in the case of linguistic difference. Just as a broken tool can serve to light up the situation in which tools otherwise function normally, so can the breakdown of communication and the resulting need for translation serve to illuminate the situation in which, otherwise, one converses with another or reads a text. Yet, while thus drawing out the parallels with translation that serve to illuminate the character of a conversation in which two persons come to an understanding, Gadamer also, if more subtly, lets this orientation to conversation recoil upon translation in such a way as to elucidate it along the lines of the classical determination while also exposing the limits and the distortion that have the effect of compromising this determination, of beginning to undermine it.

To an extent Gadamer grants the restitution or preservation of meaning that is central to the classical determination. Yet he stresses equally that translation, in preserving the meaning, transposes it into a different context. Here is his formulation in *Truth and Method*: "Here the translator must carry the meaning to be understood over into the context in which the interlocutor lives. This is not of course to say that he is at liberty to falsify the meaning intended by the speaker. Rather, the meaning is to be preserved, but, since it is to be understood in a new language world, it must establish its validity therein in a new way." Gadamer concludes: "Thus every translation is already interpretation."[26] One could say: the translator not only must intend the meaning and keep that intention in force so that the meaning is preserved in the translation but also must interpret the meaning so as to be able to set it in the context of the other language, to express it in the new language world in such a way as to establish it as a valid meaning within that world. Because the meaning must be fitted to the new context, installed within that context, it can never suffice for the would-be translator of a text only to reawaken the original psychic processes of the writer, that is, the complex of meaning-intentions borne by the original text. Rather, as Gadamer says, the translation of a text is a text formed anew, *eine Nachbildung*. Only through such *Nachbilden* can what is meant in a text be carried over into the context of another language.

And yet, every translation is like a betrayal; it is a kind of treason committed against the original text. This is what Gadamer says in a text from 1989 entitled "Lesen ist wie Übersetzen,"[27] in which his theme is not so much translatability as untranslatability. Yet this theme is already broached, if less emphatically, in *Truth and Method:* the translator, Gadamer says, must make a "constant renunciation" because, however faithful his translation may be, he cannot overcome the gulf between the two languages so as to close completely the gap between original and translation. There are always junctures where no smooth transposition is possible, where in order to emphasize one feature of the original—that is, to carry it over to the translation—other features must be played down or even suppressed. Translation occurs, then, says Gadamer, as a highlighting (*eine Überhellung*). Hence, on the one hand, a translation that takes its task seriously is always clearer than the original: expressions that in the original remain ambiguous, that bear manifold meanings, must be resolved by the translator into univocal expressions in all but those few fortunate instances in which the language

26. Gadamer, *Wahrheit und Methode*, in vol. 1 of *Gesammelte Werke*, 387–88. In linking translation to interpretation, Gadamer echoes Heidegger, who writes: "But every translation is already interpretation" (*Was Heisst Denken?*, 107).

27. Gadamer, "Lesen ist wie Übersetzen (1989)," in vol. 8 of *Gesammelte Werke*, 279.

of the translation offers expressions comparably ambiguous or manifold. But such resolution entails, on the other hand, that the translation is also flatter than the original, that—in Gadamer's phrase—"it lacks some of the overtones that vibrate in the original."[28]

Even in Schlegel's translation of Shakespeare such flatness is not entirely lacking; even in such masterly translation, highlighting cannot but have occurred with a resulting loss of some of the overtones that vibrate in Shakespeare's original text. For example, near the beginning of *A Midsummer Night's Dream* there is an exchange between the lovers Lysander and Hermia, whose love has just been interdicted by Theseus at the urgings of Hermia's father. The exchange has to do with the difficulties that true love ever encounters. It issues in a certain resolve, expressed by Hermia:

> If then true lovers have been ever cross'd,
> It stands as an edict in destiny.
> Then let us teach our trial patience,
> Because it is a customary cross,
> As due to love as thoughts and dreams and sighs,
> Wishes and tears, poor fancy's followers.
>
> (I.i.150–55)

Here is Schlegel's translation:

> Wenn Leid denn immer treue Liebe traf,
> So steht es fest im Rate des Geschicks.
> Drum lass Geduld uns durch die Prüfung lernen,
> Weil Leid der Liebe so geeignet ist
> Wie Träume, Seufzer, stille Wünsche, Tränen,
> Der armen kranken Leidenschaft Gefolge.

In the translation three instances of highlighting can be marked. In each instance the manifold sense of the original is resolved into a more nearly univocal sense, rendering the translation thus flatter than the original, robbing the text of some of its overtones.

The first instance has to do with that which true lovers ever encounter. Shakespeare's text calls it being "cross'd." No doubt the

28. Gadamer, *Wahrheit und Methode*, 390.

word alludes to crucifixion, hence to pain, to suffering. But to be "cross'd" also means to be opposed by someone or by some force, to meet opposition that hinders what one desires or intends. It means also, consequently, to be frustrated by such hindering of one's intent. Such opposition and the resulting frustration are precisely what Lysander and Hermia have experienced. Yet Schlegel resolves these manifold senses into a single one: what true lovers—or rather, true love (*treue Liebe*)—encounter or undergo is pain and suffering (*Leid*). And what Shakespeare's text calls "a customary cross" becomes in the translation the suffering that is proper to love. In another passage, just a few lines earlier, in which Hermia refers to the cross:

> O cross! too high to be enthrall'd to low[,]
>
> (I.i.136)

the word is rendered as *Qual* (agony, suffering). Here too, then, the translation produces a flattening and even a certain literalizing of the original.

In the second instance the flattening is produced in a different way. It occurs in the rendering of the names of those other things that are as proper to love as is being cross'd. Shakespeare's text lists five such things: thoughts, dreams, sighs, wishes, and tears. Schlegel's translation lists only four, omitting *thoughts;* it also silences the wishes of the lovers (*stille Wünsche*). Consequently, it orients the description of love's deeds to mute passion; this is one possibility in Shakespeare's text but by no means the only one.

The reductions culminate in the third instance. It is a matter of naming that which all those things proper to love follow, that which leads and governs them. In Shakespeare's text its name is *fancy*. It is called *poor* fancy, though not because it is weak or impotent but rather quite the contrary: because it is so powerfully operative and yet is deprived of that which it envisions, cross'd in its imagined intent. Schlegel's translation, on the other hand, calls this leader of love's deeds by the name already suggested by the previous reductions: it is a *Leidenschaft* (passion) that not only is poor (*arm*) but also is ailing, ill (*krank*), presumably because of its lack of satisfaction. The reduction is here especially decisive: by replacing *fancy* with the translation of *passion*, Schlegel obliterates the all-important reference to phantasy and imagination, which figure so thoroughly in the play as a whole. It is because lovers' deeds are governed by phantastical vision that their loves can be cross'd, as when Puck squeezes the magic juice on their eyelids. It is precisely such vision that becomes thematic in Theseus' speech on imagination at the beginning of the final Act. In the operation of the lover's fancy, passion is no doubt involved, is generated in the sight—actual or imaginary—of the beloved. But fancy thoroughly exceeds mute passion. It is also the creative vision that, as Theseus says,

> . . . bodies forth
> The forms of things unknown. . . .
>
> (V.i.14–15)

And it can command a power of speech that

> . . . gives to airy nothing
> A local habitation and a name.
>
> (V.i.16–17)

The risk of inordinately flattening and distorting a text in its translation is all the greater when the difference between the two languages is more extreme. In such cases the difference between various translations of an original into one and the same language or into closely related languages is also likely to be greater. This difference between various translations is especially striking when it is found in translations of classical texts that have undergone multiple retranslation over a considerable span of time as well as the stabilizing effect that extensive commentary and interpretation can have.

The first sentence of Plato's *Phaedo* is sounded in the voice of Echecrates, a citizen of Phlius, a city in the Peloponnesus to which the news about the details of Socrates' death had not yet traveled. Echecrates puts his question to Phaedo, who has recently arrived from Athens. Echecrates wants to know whether Phaedo was present at the scene of Socrates' death or whether he heard about it from someone else. When Phaedo responds that he was there himself, Echecrates asks him to tell about what was said and done there. It is this narrative by Phaedo that constitutes almost the entire dialogue.

Echecrates' opening question reads as follows: "Αὐτός, ὦ Φαίδων, παρεγένου Σωκράτει ἐκείνῃ τῇ ἡμέρᾳ, ᾗ τὸ φάρμακον ἔπιεν ἐν τῷ δεσμωτηρίῳ, ἢ ἄλλου του ἤκουσας;" Hackforth's English translation is fairly typical: "Were you there yourself, Phaedo, with Socrates on the day when he drank the poison in the prison, or did you hear the story from someone else?"[29] Also fairly typical is Schleiermacher's German rendering: "Warest du selbst, o Phaidon, bei dem Sokrates an jenem Tage, als er das Gift trank in dem Gefängnis, oder hast du es von einem andern gehört?"[30] In these translations of this sentence there are two somewhat distinct kinds of highlighting at work; both have the effect of flattening the text, of closing off possibilities, of resolving multiplicities that remain intact as such in the original.

One such translational operation is exercised on the phrase ᾗ τὸ φάρμακον ἔπιεν ("when he drank the poison," according to the typical translations). What is at stake here is the word φάρμακον. Certainly the word can mean *poison*. Typical translations take it for granted that since at the end of the dialogue Socrates dies from having drunk the φάρμακον the word simply designates *poison*. But in fact the word also can mean *drug, medicine, remedy*; φάρμακον νόσου means a *medicine* or *remedy for a disease*. If one is attentive to Socrates' final words about a debt owed to Asclepius, the physician god to whom it was customary to sacrifice a cock upon recovering from an illness or disease, then it hardly seems outrageous to keep this second signification (as medicine,

29. Plato, *Phaedo*, trans. R. Hackforth (Indianapolis: Bobbs-Merrill, n.d.), 27. Fowler's version is similar: "Were you with Socrates yourself, Phaedo, on the day when he drank the poison in prison, or did you hear about it from someone else?" (Plato, *Euthyphro, Apology, Crito, Phaedo, Phaedrus*, trans. H. N. Fowler, Loeb Classical Library [Cambridge, Mass.: Harvard University Press, 1914], 201).

30. Platon, *Phaidon*, trans. F. Schleiermacher, in vol. 4 of *Sämtliche Werke* (Frankfurt a.M.: Insel, 1991), 191. Zehnpfennig's version is similar: "Warst du selbst, Phaidon, bei Sokrates an jenem Tag, als er im Gefängnis das Gift trank, oder hast du es von einem anderen gehört?" (Platon, *Phaidon*, trans. Barbara Zehnpfennig [Hamburg: Felix Meiner, 1991], 3).

remedy) in play, as the word φάρμακον does but as the typical translation *poison* does not. Indeed one can easily find translations that—based on the confidence that the main point is just Socrates' execution—obscure both senses. Thus Tredennick simply renders the phrase ᾗ τὸ φάρμακον ἔπιεν as: "when he was executed"[31]—dropping all reference to the φάρμακον and to Socrates' drinking it, flattening the phrase to the point of nonrecognition. But there is still a third sense of the word φάρμακον: an *enchanted potion* or *philtre* and, linked to this, a *charm* or *enchantment*. If one anticipates the preoccupation, expressed later in the dialogue, with charming away the fear of death, then it is less than outrageous to suppose that even this third sense is in play when the word φάρμακον occurs in the opening sentence. What is needed is a translation that retains all three senses that are in play in the Greek word. The translation by Brann, Kalkavage, and Salem comes closest to filling this need by rendering φάρμακον as *potion*.[32]

The second kind of highlighting reduction that one finds in translations of the opening sentence of the *Phaedo* has to do, not with the multiplicity of meanings of words, but with syntax, specifically with word order. In general it is well known that in translating a sentence from classical Greek into a modern European language, one is usually compelled to alter the word order quite thoroughly in order to produce a translation that not only is fluent but also expresses the meaning of the sentence as a whole. But it is also known—if less widely—that in most Platonic dialogues the very first sentence is among the most significant, in many cases announcing a theme, a question, or a directionality that governs the entire dialogue. In some cases this announcement is borne primarily by the very first word, as with the word κατέβην ("I went down") at the very beginning of the *Republic*.[33] The *Phaedo* is

31. Plato, *Phaedo*, trans. Hugh Tredennick, in *The Collected Dialogues of Plato*, ed. Edith Hamilton and Huntington Cairns (Princeton: Princeton University Press, 1961), 41.

32. Plato, *Phaedo*, trans. Eva Brann, Peter Kalkavage, and Eric Salem (Newburyport, Mass.: Focus Publishing/R. Pullins Company, 1998), 27.

33. See my discussion in *Being and Logos*, 313–20.

also such a case. With its very first word, αὐτός, it announces the question that will occupy the entire dialogue. At the outset the question is enacted in this initial word: What is spoken of when, addressing Phaedo, Echecrates says, or rather asks about, *yourself?* What is the self of Phaedo or of any person? Is it the soul or the body or both? More generally, what does it mean for something to be itself? In the most rigorous sense it means not being anything other than itself, being identical with itself, being the same as itself; indeed the word αὐτός can also mean, in a certain syntactical connection: *same*. The first word of the dialogue thus alludes to a kind of being that is the same as itself; when the dialogue, at several crucial junctures, comes to speak of such beings, the names that will be used for them are ἰδέα and εἶδος.

With the first sentence of the *Phaedo*, at least with the beginning of the sentence, there is need, then, to preserve the word order, even if, as in the typical translations cited above, altering the word order produces a smoother, more fluent sentence in English or German. Again it is the translation by Brann, Kalkavage, and Salem that fulfills this need: "You yourself, Phaedo—were you present with Socrates on that day when he drank the potion in the prison, or did you hear from somebody else?"

Once Phaedo has explained what caused the long delay of Socrates' execution, Echecrates is keen to hear all about what took place at the scene of Socrates' death. He implores Phaedo to give a full and exact report: "Ταῦτα δὴ πάντα προθυμήθητι ὡς σαφέστατα ἡμῖν ἀπαγγεῖλαι, . . ."[34] Fowler translates: "Be so good as to tell us as exactly as you can about all these things, . . ."[35] Hackforth renders it: "Well, please do your best to give us a reliable report, . . ."[36] Schleiermacher: "Alles dieses bemühe dich doch uns recht genau zu erzählen, . . ."[37] However, with phrases such as "Be so good as to," "Do your best to give us," and "Bemühe dich doch," these translations all fail to keep open the sense of

34. Plato, *Phaedo* 58d.

35. Plato, *Euthyphro, etc.*, trans. H. N. Fowler, 203.

36. Plato, *Phaedo*, trans. R. Hackforth, 28.

37. Platon, *Phaidon*, trans. F. Schleiermacher, 193.

προθυμήθητι, from προθυμέομαι. While the word can indeed be said to mean *to be ready, willing, to do* a thing, such a rendering leaves out of account the inclusion in this word of the word θυμός, which can mean *heart, soul, spirit* and which in the *Republic* is the name given to that part of the soul that mediates between calculation and desire. Only the translation by Brann, Kalkavage, and Salem manages to retain this component in what otherwise seems a rather commonplace word: "Well, put your heart into giving us as sure a report as you can about all these things, . . ."[38]

If even the most masterful translations will always have been compelled by the force of linguistic difference to choose between significations that in the original are intact in their multiplicity, then translation will always involve loss.[39] By highlighting certain significations, translation will necessarily—with a necessity enforced by linguistic difference—reduce or even obliterate others, reducing them to mere overtones or silencing them altogether. In translation something of the original is lost; this is why it never suffices to translate a text into one language by translating its translation into another language. The loss incurred by translation is not, however, pure expenditure but rather, at the very least, will be situated within an economy in which the loss is compensated for by certain gains in another dimension. In translating a text one may come to a more adequate and detailed understanding of it despite the necessary reduction, or rather, in many instances, because the necessity of reduction, the operation of linguistic difference, puts in relief features of the original that would otherwise go unnoticed. There are indeed some texts, for instance, the fragments of the early Greek philosophers, that one could not interpret without also engaging in translational operations. Yet there is a return, a compensatory gain, not only for the translator but also for the reader capable of reading the text only in translation. In this

---

38. Plato, *Phaedo*, trans. Brann, Kalkavage, and Salem, 28.

39. It goes almost without saying that the extent and significance of the loss depend on the character of the text. With technical and business communications the loss is minimal and may be of no significance at all. With literary and philosophical texts, on the other hand, the loss is seldom insignificant.

connection the loss of signification would be the price of extending the range of communication.[40]

Yet loss there is. Indeed declarations and attestations of such loss through translation are ubiquitous. The case of poetry is most frequently and most vehemently invoked, even to the point of its being simply declared untranslatable.[41] Such a declaration is recorded

---

40. While it is necessary, especially as a bulwark against commodification, to place all considerations of the relation of translation to the reader within the framework of the economy just sketched, Benjamin goes too far in dismissing this relation as irrelevant to the understanding of translation and even as misleading. Observing that what is essential to a poetic work (*Dichtung*) is neither communication (*Mitteilung*) nor statement (*Aussage*), Benjamin argues that a translation determined as conveying (*vermitteln*) something to the reader would—at least in the case of a poetic work—convey nothing but a communication (*Mitteilung*), hence something quite unessential. What is essential to a poetic work, according to Benjamin, is what it contains in addition to mere communication: "the unfathomable, mysterious, 'poetic'." He concludes that as long as translation is considered as serving the reader, that is, as merely conveying a communication to the reader, it will remain bad translation, that is, "a vague transmission [*ungenaue Übermittlung*] of an unessential content" (Benjamin, "Die Aufgabe des Übersetzers," 50). In this account there are two assumptions that, if questioned, put also in question Benjamin's thesis that translation is not for the reader, a thesis that he extends also to the original of a poetic work, thus maintaining that "no poem is for the reader [*kein Gedicht gilt dem Leser*]." What is, first of all, assumed in the entire discussion is an abstract distinction between communication (i.e., what can be communicated or conveyed) and the poetic, as if a communication could not be conveyed precisely in such a way as also to bear the poetic along with it. This points in turn to the second assumption, namely, a very traditional and highly sedimented concept of the artwork as basically a thing upon which a poetic moment is grafted, that is, in the case of *Dichtung*, communicable statements endowed with a mysterious, poetic significance.

41. The great exception is Hegel, who maintains not only that it is a matter of indifference whether a poetic work is read silently or heard aloud but also that such a work "can even be translated into other languages without essential detriment to its value." It can even—without detriment, he implies—be "turned from poetry into prose" (Hegel, *Ästhetik*, ed. Friedrich Bassenge [West Berlin: das europäische buch, 1985], 2:331).

Hegel's assertion of such a reign of translatability precisely where it would least be expected, in poetry, is a direct consequence of the position he takes regarding the proper sensible element of poetry. As a form of art—even as the highest form—poetry must have a sensible element; for art as such is the *sensible*

by Boswell as having been put forth by Samuel Johnson in a conversation of 11 April 1776.[42] Boswell initiates the discussion by confessing his own inability to define translation or to illustrate what it is by means of a similitude; he suggests nonetheless that its application to poetry is limited, that "the translation of poetry could be only imitation." Johnson responds by granting that books of science can be translated exactly and that history too, except insofar as it is poetical, admits of translation. He continues: "Poetry, indeed, cannot be translated; and, therefore, it is the poets that preserve languages; for we would not be at the trouble to learn a

---

presentation of the true. But whereas one might take spoken or written words as comprising this sensible element, corresponding to the stone, color, and tone of architecture, painting, and music, Hegel insists that the proper element of poetry is inner representation and intuition itself (das *innere Vorstellen* und *Anschauen* selbst). As the painter uses color in order to present something, so the poet shapes one's inner representational powers so that one comes to intuit inwardly that which the poet would present. Speech, which might otherwise be taken as the sensible element in poetry, Hegel considers a mere sign from which one withdraws at the very start; speech exhausts itself in its capacity as a mere sign, and the sensible character of speech is not carried over to the poetic work itself; as mere sign, speech does not determine—but only communicates—the poetic work. Thus the work remains unaffected by shifts from one system of signs to another, that is, by translation.

Hegel's concept of the poetic work is grounded in the thesis, central to the *Aesthetics*, that art as such is essentially past. Indeed this essential pastness is preeminently displayed in poetry, in which the proper sensible element becomes a spiritual form (intuition), while the apparent sensible element (speech) proves to be a dispensable, external sign. In Hegel's words: "Precisely at this highest stage, art now transcends itself, in that it forsakes the element of a reconciled embodiment of the spirit in sensuous form and passes over from the poetry of representation to the prose of thought" (ibid., 1:94).

Any confrontation with Hegel's assertion of the unlimited translatability of poetry, confronting this thesis with the almost ubiquitous testimony to the contrary, would have to engage the fundamental position of Hegel's *Aesthetics* as a whole. Here it must suffice merely to formulate a question from which such an engagement might commence—namely: Can the power of inner representation or intuition, which Hegel identifies as imagination (*Phantasie*), operate in essential detachment from speech? Or is its allegedly spiritual character necessarily contaminated, as it were, by the sensible character of speech?

42. James Boswell, *Life of Johnson* (London: Oxford University Press, 1966), 742.

language, if we could have all that is written in it just as well in a translation. But as the beauties of poetry cannot be preserved in any language except that in which it was originally written, we learn the language." Clearly Johnson has in mind the classical languages, since it is only the so-called dead languages that require such preservation, that can live on only through those who learn these languages in order to read the poetry, which in turn is preserved in its beauty only within the original language.

And yet, Johnson's seemingly categorical denial of the possibility of translating poetry is moderated by what he says in other connections. For instance, in a conversation dated 9 April 1778,[43] there is mention of a recent translation of Aeschylus, a translation that is praised by one of Johnson's interlocutors but that he thinks is little more than verbiage. Asked to reconsider by reading one of the plays in this translation, Johnson enunciates the standard by which he will judge it: "We must try its effect as an English poem; that is the way to judge of the merit of a translation."

Johnson's further remark that "Translations are, in general, for people who cannot read the original" could suggest that he places little value on the enterprise of translation. And yet, two decades earlier Johnson had written in a rather different tone about translation. In *The Idler*[44] he introduces his history of translation with the declaration that of all the studies undertaken in the past three centuries "none has been more diligently or more successfully cultivated than the art of translation." Though he mentions some Roman translations of Greek poetry and grants that the Arabs "felt the ardour of translation," he regards translation as primarily something modern. He traces briefly the history of translation in England, marking the opposite extremes that for the most part had prevailed. From the time of Chaucer until that of the Restoration, the translations produced were, with few exceptions, strictly lit-

43. Ibid., 920–21.

44. Samuel Johnson, *The Idler*, in vol. 2 of *The Yale Edition of the Works of Samuel Johnson*, ed. W. J. Bate, John M. Bullitt, and L. F. Powell (New Haven: Yale University Press, 1963), 211–17 (no. 68, Saturday, 4 August 1759; no. 69, Saturday, 11 August 1759).

eral. Johnson refers to the case of Caxton, whose translations from the French are said to have followed the original so scrupulously that they were barely English: "tho' the words are English the phrase is foreign." With the Restoration, translators threw off the yoke of such "servile closeness"; yet the freedom, even licentiousness, of their translations did little more than veil "their want of learning behind the colours of a gay imagination." At best, these translations proved—for all their mistakes and negligence—more delightful to the reader.

Johnson's history of translation, displaying the opposite extremes of literalism and freedom, serves primarily to set the stage for the appeal to a mean, with which Johnson concludes: "There is undoubtedly a mean to be observed. Dryden saw very early that closeness best preserved an author's sense, and that freedom best exhibited his spirit; he therefore will deserve the highest praise who can give a representation at once faithful and pleasing, who can convey the same thoughts with the same graces, and who when he translates changes nothing but the language." Thus, following the classical determination, Johnson in effect identifies the measure of translation as restitution both of meaning ("thoughts") and of form or style ("graces"). It is because a translation ought to change nothing but the language that the merits of an English translation of a poem are to be judged by trying its effect as an English poem.

Even if one takes Johnson at his word, that "Poetry, indeed, cannot be translated," virtually all else that he says of translation appears to construe this impossibility as an impossibility of complete restitution. The restitution of thoughts and of graces will inevitably be limited, and the translator of poetry will always necessarily have changed more than just the language. Still, granted the limit, there can be excellence, even greatness, in the translation of poetry. In the conversation of 9 April 1778 concerning English translations of Greek classics, Johnson is asked about Pope's translation of Homer and declares: "Sir, it is the greatest work of the kind that has ever been produced."

From the perspective of modern linguistics, Jakobson is equally insistent that poetry cannot—at least by a certain measure—be translated. In his words: "Poetry by definition is untranslatable. Only creative transposition is possible."[45] Heidegger goes still further and extends such virtual untranslatability to thinking as well as poetry—in a remark itself barely translatable, requiring transposition: "Thinking can no more be translated than can poetry."[46] One can agree that most poetry and many philosophical texts are untranslatable if untranslatable means precisely not translatable without loss of signification, even perhaps very significant loss of signification. One can agree that such kinds of texts are untranslatable if untranslatable means that the translator will never succeed in changing nothing but the language, in effecting a pure transition from one language to the other. Yet translations there are, and though they may never be without loss, the loss and the reduction and distortion it can produce are not such as to disentitle these translations altogether. Not, at least, in the most fortunate cases: for Schlegel has produced translations of Shakespeare's poetry, as Schleiermacher and others have produced translations of Platonic dialogues, and as Heidegger himself has produced translations of passages from Greek philosophical texts. For the most part—and certainly in such exceptional instances—it is not a matter of untranslatablilty in an unconditional sense, as though any attempt at translation would inevitably fail to produce anything that could even be deemed a translation. Rather, in every instance it is a matter of a reexpression that can—and often does—succeed to some degree, but—at least in the case of poetry—always only to some degree. Reexpressing a text in another language world requires resolving certain multiple meanings, transposing various syntactic structures, and shifting from particular

---

45. Jakobson, *Language in Literature*, 434.

46. "So wenig wie man Gedichte übersetzen kann, kann man ein Denken übersetzen" (Heidegger, "Spiegel-Gespräch," in *Antwort: Martin Heidegger im Gespräch*, ed. G. Neske and E. Kettering [Pfullingen: Günther Neske, 1988], 108). Another passage simply declares poetry untranslatable: "Translation and translation are not the same if it is a matter, on the one hand, of a business letter and, on the other hand, of a poem. The one is translatable; the other is not" (Heidegger, *Der Satz vom Grund*, 163).

metaphorics valid in the one language to other metaphorics valid in the other language, hence reexpressing certain figures of the original within an alien metaphorics appropriate to the other language. Such reductions, transpositions, and shifts result in loss of signification and of syntactical and metaphorical force, and this is why translation of poetic or philosophical texts can succeed only to some degree. It is in this sense that such texts may be called untranslatable.

Such texts involve, then, a certain untranslatability, which is attested by the loss sustained in translating them. In some cases a loss can be discerned with remarkable clarity in the translation of proper names. Such names are as such meaningless, and for the most part they function in discourse without becoming meaningful. Even when, as in *A Midsummer Night's Dream*, a name such as Theseus invokes a historical or mythical character, it does so by referring to something singular rather than by signifying a general meaning. It is for this reason that a proper name does not belong to a particular language with the same insistence that other words do; and it is also for this reason that a translator between languages as closely related as English and German can simply carry over many of the proper names unaltered. Except for their historical or mythical associations, these names have virtually no relation to meaning and thus have little bearing on the meaning, the complex of meaning, that the translator is to preserve in the translation. Yet there are exceptions, certain names that both name and signify and that have therefore a marginal or oblique bearing on the complex of meaning. In some cases the proper name signifies by coinciding with some generic designation: as with the characters Mustardseed, Wall, Moonshine, and Lion. In such instances the translation can straightforwardly render the generic designations: as does Schlegel in rendering these as Senfsamen, Wand, Mondschein, and Löwe. But there are other names that are related to meaning in more subtle and complex ways; these are the tag-names that Shakespeare weaves into the fabric of his plays in such masterly ways. In such cases the name not only indicates an individual character but also through its meaning can bear, for instance, on the very character that it also names. In *A Midsummer*

Night's Dream a prime instance is the name *Bottom*. Bottom is a weaver, and his name in effect signifies his profession, since in Elizabethan English the word *bottom* designates a kind of frame used in weaving. Both the identification of Bottom as a weaver and the allusion of his name to weaving anticipate his deeds in the play, not only that of weaving words together in a peculiar way (as when he says: "the eye of man hath not heard, the ear of man hath not seen, man's hand is not able to taste, his tongue to conceive, nor his heart to report, what my dream was" [IV.i.209–12]) but also that of weaving together the human world and the fairy world, as when he is whisked off to the bower of the fairy queen. Through another of its meanings the name *Bottom* associates the character it names with the ass whose head he acquires through Puck's mischief, with the ass's head that, atop Bottom's body, provokes Peter Quince's exclamation:

> Bless thee, Bottom, bless thee! Thou art translated.
>
> (III.i.113–14)

Translated he is indeed in Schlegel's translation of the play. When Nick Bottom becomes Klaus Zettel, his name retains, to be sure, its reference to his profession as a weaver (in the various ways he carries it on in the play), for the word *Zettel*, like *Bottom*, alludes as a common noun to weaving. On the other hand, the translation effaces the direct association of the name with the ass's head. The double meaning with which the proper name *Bottom* is associated when taken as a common noun does not survive the translation and the resolution it requires. In this regard a significant semantic component is lost in the translation.

Other losses can occur in translation, loss with respect to other moments of the original discourse. Nietzsche stresses that one of the things most easily lost in translation is the *tempo* of the style of the original. Nietzsche says that "there are honestly meant translations that . . . are almost falsifications of the original, merely because its bold and merry *tempo* (which leaps over and obviates all dangers in things and words) could not be translated." In this connection Nietzsche celebrates, at the expense of Germans and their language, the very language in which nonetheless Nietzsche writes the celebration—Nietzsche celebrates Machiavelli: "How could the German language . . . imitate the *tempo* of Machiavelli, who in his *Principe* lets us breathe the dry, refined air of Florence and cannot help presenting the most serious matters in a boisterous *allegrissimo*. . . ." Above all, Nietzsche celebrates Aristophanes, indeed to such an extent that he forgoes even broaching the question of the impossible translation of Aristophanes' tempo into German (which he calls, in a performative contradiction, "ponderous, viscous, and solemnly clumsy"); instead he veers off toward another, very heterogeneous kind of translation—if one can still call it that—by Aristophanes' great contemporary and rival: "And as for Aristophanes—that transfiguring, complementary spirit for whose sake one *forgives* everything Hellenic for having existed, provided one has understood in its full profundity *all* that needs to be forgiven and transfigured here—there is nothing that has caused me to meditate more on *Plato's* secrecy and sphinx nature than the happily preserved *petit fait* that under the pillow of his deathbed there was found no 'Bible,' nor anything Egyptian, Pythagorean, or Platonic—but a volume of Aristophanes. How could even Plato have endured life—a Greek life he repudiated—without an Aristophanes?"[47]

There are, then, various kinds of losses, losses that can be—and often are—undergone with respect to various moments of discourse. Several have been marked: loss of multiple meanings through resolution that retains only some while excluding others; loss through transposition of syntactic structures, which can obliterate, for instance, the significance that a certain word order has for the discourse; loss of metaphorical forcefulness as a result of the necessity of shifting from metaphorics valid in the original language to those valid in the other language; and loss of the tempo of the style of the original. These various kinds of loss do not for the most part operate independently. Loss of semantic components, for instance, may prove to be precisely what necessitates

---

47. Nietzsche, *Jenseits von Gut und Böse*, in vol. VI 2 of *Werke: Kritische Gesamtausgabe*, §28.

a shift of metaphorics and the loss this entails. And the transposition of syntactic structures required by the language into which a translation is made can result in a loss of the tempo of the original.

Loss there is indeed, or rather, various kinds of loss, loss with respect to various moments of the original discourse. And yet, the question imposes itself, a question that, it seems, needs especially to be posed today so as to mark the limit of—if not to undo—a certain pathos of the end of philosophy, the question whether in translation there is only loss, whether even in the translation of Greek philosophical language into Latin and hence into the modern European languages there was only loss. Or whether, at the very least, this translation served to open possibilities in the Latin language that would otherwise never have been offered, possibilities in turn passed on in some degree to the modern European languages. It is a question of whether, in Schlegel's translation of Shakespeare, there is not something gained for the German language, possibilities of sense that the language would otherwise not offer, that hitherto it did not offer—indeed in a way parallel to that in which through the poetry of Hölderlin and Goethe new possibilities of sense were opened up. Benjamin's affirmation of such translational gain for the language as such is emphatic: considered as translators, "Luther, Voss, Hölderlin, and George have extended the boundaries of the German language." In this regard Benjamin cites Pannwitz, for whom translation's transformation of one's own language takes the form of an imperative to which few translators have measured up: "The basic error of the translator is that he holds onto the chance condition of his own language instead of letting his language be powerfully moved by the foreign language. . . . He must extend and deepen his language by means of the foreign language."[48]

Yet, even beyond what can be gained for a language as such by the effect that translation can have upon it, is it possible for translation to bring about—even if without simply canceling the loss—a certain gain in the work translated? Gadamer grants that there

48. Benjamin, "Die Aufgabe des Übersetzers," 60–61.

are rare instances in which the translator succeeds in compensating for the loss by balancing it with a comparable gain or even by producing such gain as exceeds the loss. He mentions, though without elaboration, the case of George's translation of Baudelaire's *Les Fleurs du Mal*.[49] Yet one cannot but wonder about the possibility of such gain, or rather, about what precisely could constitute such gain. If indeed translation preserves the meaning expressed in the original, merely transposing that same meaning into another linguistic context, then the gain could not be a gain in meaning, could not be an accrual of additional meaning to the original meaning. The gain, it seems, could only be one of expression; it could only be a matter of expressing the meaning to a greater degree in the translation as compared with the original. But what is this greater degree of expression? And does such expression to a greater degree remain, as it seems it must, distinct from the meaning that it, to a greater degree than the original, expresses?

Expression to a greater degree may be achieved by virtue of the metaphoricity of the translation, by an enhancement of the figures of expression. Translating any poetic text requires engagement with the metaphorics of the text if the forcefulness and expressiveness of the figures are to be carried over to the translation. In many instances what is required is a shift of metaphorics, or rather the unfolding or composition of a metaphorics that in the language of the translation can come near matching in expressiveness the corresponding metaphorics in the original. For example, in the exchange between Lysander and Hermia near the beginning of *A Midsummer Night's Dream*, the exchange in which they speak of the difficulties that true love ever encounters, there is a passage in which Lysander surveys the various ways in which love can all too soon be brought to an end. The passage concludes as follows:

> And, ere a man hath power to say 'Behold!',
> The jaws of darkness do devour it up:
> So quick bright things come to confusion.
>
> (I.i.147–49)

---

49. Gadamer, *Wahrheit und Methode*, 390.

Schlegel translates:

> Doch eh' ein Mensch vermag zu sagen: schaut!
> Schlingt gierig ihn die Finsternis hinab:
> So schnell verdunkelt sich des Glückes Schein.

The metaphorical shift is evident in the final line: that which, according to Shakespeare's text, comes to confusion is said—countertranslating Schlegel's rendering—to grow dark. Thus, in place of the metaphorics of confusion, that is, of a disturbance that weakens or destroys the composition of something by mixing up, jumbling together, what belongs to it, Schlegel inscribes a metaphorics of darkening, setting this off against Shakespeare's expression *bright things* (and his own word *Schein*) but also carrying it over from Shakespeare's expression *jaws of darkness* in the previous line. Even though it would not have been impossible to retain the original's metaphorics of confusion, translating this as *Verwirrung* (*Sprachverwirrung* means *confusion of tongues*, as in the story of Babel), Schlegel's shift of the metaphorics links the final line to the previous one and allows him to interpret Shakespeare's *bright things* as *des Glückes Schein*, as the light or shining of good fortune or of love's happiness, since something that is lighted or that shines can subsequently grow dark but cannot as such come to confusion. Thus, on the one hand, it could be said that Schlegel's shift of the metaphorics has the effect of flattening the text metaphorically by reducing what form two metaphorics in Shakespeare's original to the single metaphorics of darkening. Yet, on the other hand, the shift can be regarded as consolidating and hence strengthening the metaphorics and as making it possible to enhance the specificity of Shakespeare's *bright things*. At least in this regard there is good reason to say that the translation makes a gain over the original, even if, regarded otherwise, there is loss with respect to the original.

In the shifting of metaphorics, whether enforced by linguistic difference or prompted by other concerns, something that always must be taken into account is the resonance of the relevant figure with other metaphorical figures in the same discourse. Such resonances between figures become all the more significant for the discourse as a whole when these figures are rigorously bound to a conceptuality; in no other discourses is this more thoroughly the case than in the Platonic dialogues, at least if allowance is made (and this, too, is a problem of translation) for the fact that the concept, as it were, of the concept is not yet intact or decided in these discourses. One could suppose, then, that the resonances are nowhere more significant than in those passages in the dialogues where certain figures are rigorously bound not just to a conceptuality but to the very origination of conceptuality as such. One such passage occurs in the *Phaedo* at the point where Socrates has just finished telling of his efforts to investigate nature, efforts that failed and that left him bereft of even the knowledge he had formerly thought secure. It is against this background that Socrates then proposes to tell his interlocutors how he went on to venture a quite different kind of inquiry, the kind of inquiry that had eventually provoked such opposition that Socrates found himself condemned to death. As he is awaiting death there in the prison cell with his closest friends, he tells of his δεύτερος πλοῦς.

Tredennick's translation, "makeshift approach,"[50] simply demetaphorizes the phrase, ignoring the fact that δεύτερος πλοῦς designates the kind of sailing that one must venture when there is no wind and it becomes necessary to resort to the oars. Even if one can say that such a means of sailing is in a sense makeshift, this does not entail that it is something just randomly taken up, for it is a means always available and always to be relied upon in such situations. Although Hackforth's rendering, "second-best method,"[51] avoids suggesting randomness, it still strips the expression of its metaphoricity. Schleiermacher's rendering, "zweitbeste Fahrt," Zehnpfennig's "zweite Fahrt," and Fowler's "second voyage"[52] adhere a bit more to the metaphoricity of the expression. Yet still, the word πλοῦς (linked to πλέω, *to sail*, and πλοῖον, *ship*) does not designate just any kind of voyage (*Fahrt*) but only a sea voyage, a voyage by ship, sailing. Hence the most accurate rendering, the one that adheres to the metaphoricity of the expression,

50. Plato, *Phaedo*, trans. Hugh Tredennick, 81.

51. Plato, *Phaedo*, trans. R. Hackforth, 127.

52. Platon, *Phaidon*, trans. F. Schleiermacher, 299; Platon, *Phaidon*, trans. Barbara Zehnpfennig, 121; Plato, *Euthyphro*, etc., trans. H. N. Fowler, 343.

is that found in the translation by Brann, Kalkavage, and Salem: "second sailing."[53]

Yet what counts most is not just the accuracy of this translation but the fact that it leaves intact the resonances of this expression with numerous others. There is, for instance, an earlier passage in which Simmias expresses his reservations about what Socrates has just declared concerning the immortality of the soul. Simmias suggests that perhaps in this life one cannot know anything sure about such matters and so "must sail through life in the midst of danger, seizing on the best and the least refutable of human discourses [λόγοι], at any rate, and let himself be carried upon it as upon a raft."[54] Yet, above and beyond this and other passages built around the metaphorical value of sailing, the most decisive resonance sustained by δεύτερος πλοῦς is with the sailings set out at the beginning of the dialogue, the mythic sailing of Theseus to Crete to slay the Minotaur and the sailing of the ship to Delos in fulfillment of a vow made to Apollo to assure Theseus' success, the sailing that has the effect of delaying Socrates' death and in this sense opening the very interval in which the discussions in the *Phaedo* take place. To say nothing of the manner in which the course of those discussions, the way followed by the dialogue itself, has the character of a nautical course.

Even in the rendering of proper names translation can produce a gain, though it does so only rarely and chiefly in the case of tag-names, which not only name but also signify something about the very thing or person named. Such a gain is registered when *Nick Bottom* becomes *Klaus Zettel*. The gain is marked in the first scene (I.ii) in which the mechanicals appear, the scene in Quince's house where they meet to be assigned the roles they are to play in the performance before Theseus and his company. As he reads off the assignments, Quince is playing already, as later, the role of director. Yet it is Bottom who instructs him how to proceed and who urges him on:

---

53. Plato, *Phaedo*, trans. Brann, Kalkavage, and Salem, 79.

54. Plato, *Phaedo* 85c–d.

You were best to call them generally, man by man, according to the scrip.

(I.ii.2–3)

Quince replies:

Here is the scroll of every man's name which is thought fit through all Athens to play in our interlude before the Duke and the Duchess, on his wedding-day at night.

(I.ii.4–7)

As soon as Quince has stated the title of the play, Bottom again urges him to read out the assignments:

Now, good Peter Quince, call forth your actors by the scroll.

(I.ii.14–15)

The first name called is that of Nick Bottom:

Answer as I call you. Nick Bottom, the weaver?

(I.ii.16)

In Schlegel's translation, on the other hand, Bottom's name has already been mentioned before Peter Quince reads it off from the list and assigns to Bottom the role of Pyramus. Or rather, the word *Zettel* has already been used as a common noun before Quince/Squenz uses it as the proper name of the character who is to play Pyramus. In Schlegel's translation Bottom/Zettel refers first to *die Liste,* which translates *the scrip:*

Es wäre am besten, ihr riefet auf einmal Mann für Mann auf, wie es die Liste gibt.

Quince/Squenz then refers to die Liste by another word, *der Zettel:*

Hier ist der Zettel von jedermanns Namen. . . .

Then Bottom/Zettel himself, urging Quince/Squenz on, speaks of der Zettel, calling his own name yet not as such, not as a proper name, calling his name before it has yet been called in the play:

Nun, guter Peter Squenz, ruf' die Acteurs nach dem Zettel auf.

It is at precisely this point that Quince/Squenz then calls the name, the proper name, of Bottom/Zettel:

> Antwortet, wie ich euch rufe!—Klaus Zettel, der Weber.

Thus, the passage is translated by Schlegel in such a way as to link Bottom/Zettel to the list, the scrip, the scroll, from which the director, Quince/Squenz, reads off the name of each of the mechanicals/actors along with the name of the character each is to play. Bottom/Zettel thus comes to be associated with writing, with the writing and production of plays and in particular with casting, which, in this very passage and as it continues, Bottom/Zettel tries to take over from Quince/Squenz. By the time he is finally called by name and by profession, Klaus Zettel, der Weber, an association has been woven that calls up the ancient figure of discourse as weaving. The association does not occur in Shakespeare's English text; yet it enhances the metaphorics of that text, compensating to a degree for the loss of association of Bottom's name with the beast with whose head he comes to be endowed.

The enhancement is even more striking in a passage near the beginning of the final Act. The passage comes just after Theseus has delivered his extended discourse on imagination as impelling the lunatic, the lover, and the poet. In this discourse Theseus draws a connection—or rather, redraws a connection operative since antiquity—between fantasy and imagination:

> Lovers and madmen have such seething brains,
> Such shaping fantasies, that apprehend
> More than cool reason ever comprehends.
> The lunatic, the lover, and the poet
> Are of imagination all compact[.]
>
> (V.i.4–8)

Schlegel's translation affirms the same connection:

> Verliebte und Verrückte
> Sind beide von so brausendem Gehirn,
> So bildungsreicher Phantasie, die wahrnimmt,
> Was nie die kühlere Vernunft begreift.

> Wahnwitzige Poeten und Verliebte
> Bestehn aus Einbildung.

The passage in question constitutes Hippolyta's response to what her newlywed husband has just said. She refers to what the four lovers have told of their night—or dream—in the forest:

> But all the story of the night told over,
> And all their minds transfigur'd so together,
> More witnesseth than fancy's images,
> And grows to something of great constancy;
> But howsoever, strange and admirable.
>
> (V.i.23–27)

Schlegel translates:

> Doch diese ganze Nachtbegebenheit,
> Und ihrer aller Sinn, zugleich verwandelt,
> Bezeugen mehr als Spiel der Einbildung.
> Es wird daraus ein Ganzes voll Bestand,
> Doch seltsam immer noch und wundervoll.

What is to be noted is the subtle shift that Schlegel introduces by rendering *fancy's images* as *Spiel der Einbildung*. In this translation there is restitution of meaning. Indeed *Einbildung* alone preserves the sense both of *image* and of *fancy* (that is, of *fantasy*), since it incorporates *Bild* and has already, in Theseus' discourse, been linked to *Phantasie*. Hence, in the translation of *fancy's images* as *Spiel der Einbildung*, *Spiel* functions purely as a signifier of a surplus of sense. Especially at this stage of the play, where reflection is carried out on the preceding events of the play and preparation then commences for the play within the play with which the play virtually concludes, the surplus of sense produced by the introduction of *Spiel* enhances the discourse significantly.[55] For one can say,

---

55. The production of a surplus of sense through the introduction of *Spiel* is perhaps even more conspicuous in Schlegel's translation of a later passage. The passage occurs in one of the conversations in which Theseus and his company, in the course of the performance of "Pyramus and Thisbe," exchange comments about it. In particular, when Hippolyta exclaims:

countertranslating: beyond its opening, the entire play has up to this point been a matter of play and of play of imagination, indeed a play within the play even before the commencement, in the final Act, of the play within the play that is performed by the mechanicals, the play "Pyramus and Thisbe." So thoroughly has everything become a matter of play that even the mechanicals,

> A crew of patches, rude mechanicals,
> That work for bread upon Athenian stalls,
>
> (III.ii.9–10)

have become players in a play.

In bad translations, too, there is often a surplus of sense produced; but in such cases the surplus is at odds with the sense of the original and has the effect of distorting and destabilizing the translation. With Schlegel's rendering of *fancy's images* as *Spiel der Einbildung* it is quite otherwise. Here the surplus enhances the metaphorics that governs this entire portion of the play, the metaphorics of fantasy and imagination, the metaphorics that Theseus puts in play so as to say what he has to say about fantasy and imagination. This is a metaphorics that turns toward its very origin, toward those forces capable of the originary displacement of sense through which metaphors and systems of metaphors (metaphorics) are—even if never from a simple beginning—constituted. The surplus produced by Schlegel's introduction of *Spiel* into his

---

This is the silliest stuff that ever I heard[,]

(V.i.207)

Theseus responds:

> The best in this kind are but shadows; and the worst are no worse, if imagination amend them.
>
> (V.i.208–209)

Schlegel's translation introduces *Spiel*, corresponding to nothing in Shakespeare's English text, and couples it again, if less directly, with *Einbildung*, or rather, now, with *Einbildungskraft*:

> Das beste in dieser Art ist nur Schattenspiel, und das schlechteste ist nichts schlechteres, wenn die Einbildungskraft nachhilft.

translation enhances this metaphorics by bringing the figure of play to bear on the operation of imagination. More broadly, the introduction of the figure of play contributes a decisive moment to the metaphorics within which the play and the play within the play are determined as such, as plays, as enactments in which everything is only as it seems and not as it actually is, in which everything is translated into something else and everyone into someone other. Even in what one would like to consider play in a proper, nonmetaphorical sense, for instance, the play of children, translation and metaphor are the decisive constituents. In play even in its would-be proper sense, translation and metaphor are already in play.

The insight behind Schlegel's translation of *fancy's images* as *Spiel der Einbildung*, or rather, the insight that, perhaps covertly, guides that translation, is the following: that bringing the figure of play to bear on imagination brings about an enhancement of a discourse that would turn back toward the origin of metaphoricity and translation. Translation, in particular, would seem to have no other recourse than play of imagination. From a word in one language or from the meaning of this word, one cannot infer the word in another language that will convey the same meaning. Neither is translation a matter of judgment in the classical sense of subsuming a particular under a universal; for the relation between particular and universal is a quite different relation from that between a signifier and its meaning. Because translation deals with a relation neither simply between meanings nor between meanings and singular things but rather between meanings and words, it requires a power of another kind than reason and judgment. Because translation engages a movement neither simply from word to meaning nor from meaning to word but rather, as Figal has shown,[56] a double movement from the sphere of one's own language into that of a foreign language and back from the foreign to one's own, translation requires something more than simply the

56. Günter Figal, "Seinserfahrung und Übersetzung: Hermeneutische Überlegungen zu Heidegger," *Studia Philosophica* 57 (1998): 184.

power of intention and expression. Translation cannot but have recourse to imagination, for it is imagination—especially as it came to be determined by Kant, Fichte, and the German Romantics (to whose circle A. W. Schlegel belonged)—that has the capacity to mediate between alien spheres without reducing the foreignness of their relation. Imagination is the force of holding them together in their difference, of holding them together by its movement between them, by its hovering between them.[57]

Gadamer's discussion of translation, oriented to the analysis of conversation or dialogue, becomes perhaps most incisive at those points where a certain analysis of conversation is turned back upon translation so as to clarify it. Thus, in *Truth and Method* Gadamer deals with the back and forth, the to and fro (*Hin und Her*), that is characteristic of conversation and then indicates how this character pertains also to translation: "And, as in conversation, when there are such unbridgeable differences, a compromise can sometimes be achieved in the to and fro of dialogue, so the translator will seek the best solution in the to and fro of weighing and considering [*im Hin und Her des Wägens und Erwägens*]—a solution that can never be more than a compromise."[58] It is to such a to and fro movement, a hovering, that imagination is peculiarly suited. And it is in this regard, as a free oscillation to and fro between various different terms, that imagination deploys its force as *play of imagination*. It is to such play of imagination that translation cannot but have recourse.

Even though, according to the classical determination, it is imperative that translation circulate through the meaning of the linguistic unit being translated, it is not the meaning that gets translated but the linguistic unit (the word, the phrase, the sentence). Because it is a matter of translating a word (for instance) in a foreign language into a word in one's own language (or, less commonly, the opposite), translation requires a spanning of the linguistic difference, a persisting in the alterity. Yet it requires a to and fro not only between languages but also within the language

57. See *Force of Imagination*, esp. chap. 2.

58. Gadamer, *Wahrheit und Methode*, 390.

into which one is translating, a to and fro in which one hovers between various translations that freely and imaginatively offer themselves, for they cannot be inferred or in any such way determined. On the other hand, they must be weighed and considered, tested in their capacity to express the meaning signified by the word being translated. This testing, this measuring of their force of expression, requires that the free play of imagination be bound to the intentional and expressive powers, to the very power of speech as such. For if the playful hovering of imagination between the various translations that offer themselves is to issue in a translation, these possibilities must be measured; the expressive force of each, its capacity to express the meaning expressed by the word being translated, must be measured against the others and, above all, against what is expressed by the word being translated. It is because of this measuring and the intentional-expressive powers it involves that the play of imagination in translation may be called a lawful play and that one may refer in this connection to the free lawfulness of the imagination, a lawfulness without a law.[59] Indeed, turning within the circle, one will insist that translational possibilities can offer themselves only to the free lawfulness of imagination, only to a free play of imagination that also is bound to the intentional animation of the sense of the word being translated.

Schlegel's translation of *fancy's images* as *Spiel der Einbildung* produces a surplus, a certain gain over the original, which, however, enhances the metaphorics of the original so as to make the translation in this respect more expressive. But what about such gains? Do they indeed go no further than to enhance the expressiveness of the translation, to make it express better—more forcefully—the same meaning that the original expresses? Is this the limit of the advance that Schlegel achieves by translating *fancy's images* as *Spiel der Einbildung*, by introducing into the translation the surplus of sense conveyed by *Spiel*? Is it in this case only a matter of expressing bet-

---

59. The sense of lawful play is discussed already in Plato's *Republic* (424e–425a) (see *Being and Logos*, 21–22). The designation "the free lawfulness of the imagination" and its characterization as "a lawfulness without a law" are developed in Kant's *Critique of Judgment* (*Kritik der Urteilskraft*, 240–41).

ter in German a complex of meanings that define imagination/fantasy and that would remain completely invariant as such in the translation? In a certain respect it is unquestionable that what Schlegel achieves here goes beyond mere enhancement of the expression of an invariant meaning: by bringing *Spiel* into play in the translation Schlegel makes the translation say something about imagination that is not said in Shakespeare's text. And yet, how can this surplus be produced in the translation, how can something be said that is not said in the original, without altering the meaning of the original, that is, without distorting it, that is, without, in the end, simply producing a bad translation? Is it possible to sequester the invariant original meaning, to immunize it against the intrusion of a surplus, to consign this surplus to a sphere of mere expression exterior to the meaning that translation is to preserve? Or is it perhaps the very concept of meaning that needs here to be put into question? Can translation—especially when it is a case of such a genius of translation as Schlegel—be understood as the mere recontextualizing of one and the same meaning? Does the primary responsibility of the translator lie only in the preservation—in the pure reexpression—of such meaning?

What about meaning as such? What about the concept of meaning? There is perhaps nothing more resistant to being put into question. For precisely what one intends as a question putting meaning in question—as in the questions just posed—will almost invariably prove to be nothing more than sheer tautology, which thus fails entirely to open what one calls (tautologically) meaning as such to questioning and, instead, merely repeats the same, as if compulsively, indeed under a compulsion stemming from the beginning of philosophy. For *meaning*, *what*, *as such*, and *concept* all say the same, and any configuration of them results only in tautology.

Yet, even short of such abysmal complications, there are others that are pertinent, complications pertaining specifically to translation, complications that occur in the circulation in and as which translation takes place. For the question is whether translation is a pure circulation through meaning. Two kinds of entanglements may be mentioned that have the effect of complicating the would-be pure circulation.

The first is a certain nonreciprocity that sometimes occurs in translation. The pertinent instances are not those in which a word or phrase is so poorly translated as to make it difficult to countertranslate, to translate back from the translation to the original. Rather, it is a matter of instances in which the fecundity of the translation makes possible a development that would never have been possible starting from the original. In such an instance the development has the effect of making successful countertranslation impossible—that is, the original word or phrase will prove to be inadequate as a translation of the very word or phrase into which it was translated. For example, in his essay on λόγος in Heraclitus, Heidegger ventures to translate the verb λέγειν by *lesen* in the sense of *sammeln*.[60] In turn, the English translation renders this sense by the word *to gather* or *gathering*.[61] Not only is this translation appropriate but, most significantly, the semantic and metaphorical possibilities that it opens up allow the reflection that Heidegger begins in his essay to be developed to the point where *gathering* could no longer be translated, without further ado, back into *Sammeln*.[62] What the translation enables here quite exceeds merely preserving one and the same meaning. Here it is not a matter of one and the same meaning simply persisting intact through the translation; rather, it is a matter of a translation that, without falsifying the original, enhances the meaning and opens it to mutation and transformation.

The second kind of entanglement is what might be called overtranslation. This can occur in texts in which a certain basic word or phrase undergoes a mutation of sense as a result of theoretical developments carried out in the text. Overtranslation occurs when such a word or phrase is, from the very beginning of the text, translated in such a way that in its translated form it signifies the mutated sense reached only through the developments in the

60. Heidegger, "Logos (Heraklit, Fragment 50)," in *Vorträge und Aufsätze* (Pfullingen: Günther Neske, 1954), 207–29. See esp. 209–10.

61. The translation is by David Krell, in Heidegger, *Early Greek Thinking* (New York: Harper & Row, 1975), 59–78. See especially 61–62.

62. See *The Gathering of Reason* (Athens, Ohio: Ohio University Press, 1980) and especially the Translator's Note to the German translation: *Die Krisis der Vernunft: Metaphysik und das Spiel der Einbildungskraft* (Hamburg: Felix Meiner, 1983).

text. One result of overtranslation is to render this development incoherent, trivial, or even imperceptible, since the development is already tacitly built into the translation from the beginning. On the other hand, if overtranslation is recognized as such, it can—like a broken tool—serve to illuminate something, namely, a certain operation of textuality that exceeds mere transition between stable, preconstituted meanings, an operation by which a text can produce a mutation in the very meanings that it is engaged in signifying.

In the course of Plato's *Sophist*, the Stranger arrives at a kind of definition of being. What he says at this point might be translated as follows: "For I set up as a limit [ὅρος] by which to delimit [ὁρίζειν] beings [τὰ ὄντα] that they are nothing but δύναμις."[63] But if, from the beginning of the dialogue, one had already built this definition into the translation, if, for instance, one had translated τὰ ὄντα as *capable beings* or *potential beings*, then it would not be possible even to translate this passage without rendering it tautological, to say nothing of the effect on earlier passages in the text.

Much the same bind can easily arise in translating certain of Heidegger's texts, perhaps most notably the unpublished treatises from the late 1930s and early 1940s. The radicality of these writings is such that their language is formed and deformed within the text itself, often in a kind of mutational repetition that sets words apart from the constituted language of metaphysics, that recomposes them at or beyond the limit. Heidegger himself gives an important indication in a marginal note to *Vom Wesen der Wahrheit*, in which he lays out the stages of the mutation that the sense of *Wesen* undergoes in and through that text.[64] Nothing could be less true to Heidegger's text than to incorporate that development preemptively in the very translation of *Wesen*.

Nonreciprocal translation and overtranslation serve to expose a mutation of meaning brought about either in and through the

---

63. Plato, *Sophist*, 247e.

64. The marginal note is to the third edition, 1954. It reads: "Wesen: 1. quidditas—das Was—κοινόν; 2. Ermöglichung—Bedingung der Möglichkeit; 3. Grund der Ermöglichung" (Heidegger, *Wegmarken*, vol. 9 of *Gesamtausgabe* [Frankfurt a.M.: Vittorio Klostermann, 1976], 177).

translation or in and through the operation of the text itself. In turn, the exposure of such mutation puts in question still more decisively the requirement that translation preserve meaning, that it be limited to pure circulation, to pure reexpression of meaning. In this connection it is not only a question of translation sustaining a more complex relation to meaning but also a question of whether the very concept of meaning (with all its complications) can ever suffice for a discourse on translation.

What is remarkable about Gadamer's discourse on translation is the way in which, framed within the orbit of the classical determination, it carries that determination to the limit and thereby gestures toward another determination. The general formulations in *Truth and Method* establish the frame: translation is to preserve the meaning, though, because of the necessity of setting the meaning within a new context, translation is already interpretation and its product *eine Nachbildung*. Gadamer writes even in a way reminiscent of Hegel's stress on the appropriative power of translation: as in reading a text, so in translation, says Gadamer, it is a matter "of alienness and its conquest [*vom Fremdheit und Überwindung derselben*]."[65] Through translation one would make an otherwise alien meaning one's own. Yet in this process one's own thoughts would come into play, not simply to cancel the alienness of the text so as to appropriate it, but—as Gadamer says, drawing out the parallel between reading a text and translating it—to engage in the reawakening of the meaning of the text (*in die Wiedererweckung des Textsinnes*). But still, even if in need of being reawakened, it is as though the meaning were intact so that the fusion of horizons—which Gadamer explicitly mentions in this connection—would serve, in the end, only for its preservation and reexpression in another linguistic context.

And yet, even in *Truth and Method* there are other indications that begin to push the classical determination toward the limit. One

65. Gadamer, *Wahrheit und Methode*, 365. While retaining the double movement between the foreign and one's own, Figal emphasizes the engagement of this movement with alterity rather than its appropriation of the foreign: "One could say that translation as such is characterized by a double alterity" (Figal, "Seinserfahrung und Übersetzung," 184).

such indication lies in Gadamer's introduction of the concept of spirit (*Geist*). Specifically, he characterizes the gap across which translation moves, not just as a gap between the original words and the restitution achieved in the words of another language, but rather as a gap between the *spirit* of the original words and the spirit of the restituting expression. But what is the spirit of words, of wording (*Wortlaut*), literally, of word-sounds? Is it anything other than their meaning, that which animates the sounds so that they are words and not just sounds? Even if, alternatively, one hears in Gadamer's appeal to spirit an echo of von Humboldt's idea of the spirit of a language, of a spirit unique to each language, one would still need to ponder whether meaning could remain intact apart from the various spirits of various languages, merely expressed and reexpressed according to those spirits and in those languages.

Even Gadamer's characterization of translation as highlighting (*Überhellung*) works against the classical determination by which, in *Truth and Method*, it is framed. For one could hardly suppose that those features of the original that are emphasized and those others that are played down or even suppressed have only to do with the expression of a selfsame meaning that remains completely untouched by such highlighting.

Yet it is after *Truth and Method* that a stronger thrust is exerted toward unsettling the classical determination of translation. Most notably, in the text "Lesen ist wie Übersetzen"—indeed right from the beginning of this text, with the opening citation from Croce: "Every translation is like a betrayal."[66] For a translation that purely reexpresses, if less powerfully, the meaning of the original could never be charged with betrayal, with treason, but only with weakness, imperfection, flatness. In order for every translation to be like a betrayal, translation must be such as inevitably to violate the meaning of the original; it must be such that it could never reexpress the meaning of the original. Even in this case one might of course continue to measure translation by the classical norm,

---

66. "Jede Übersetzung ist wie ein Verrat" (Gadamer, "Lesen ist wie Übersetzen," 279).

demanding that it ought to restitute the meaning though it always fails to do so, fails even necessarily and not just in fact. Yet if translation necessarily fails to achieve the result prescribed by its norm, there will be good reason to question that norm, to question whether it is the norm appropriate to translation, to question whether translation ought to be measured by the demand for restitution of meaning.

Gadamer begins to venture such questioning in the text "Lesen ist wie Übersetzen." On the one hand, he acknowledges that there are certain texts (especially of a more technical sort) where all that is important is to grasp what is meant; in such cases translation would legitimately be determined by the norm of restitution of meaning. But now Gadamer stresses how different certain other kinds of texts are, most notably, though not only, poetry. In translating, as in reading, such texts, one is engaged—says Gadamer—in "an interpretation through tone and tempo, modulation and articulation—and all this lies in the 'inner voice' and is there for the 'inner ear' of the reader."[67] Such texts are not mere expressions of meaning, but rather their very operation as texts, their textuality, also involves tone and tempo, modulation and articulation. Therefore, a translation that only restituted the meaning of such a text without recovering its inner voice would utterly betray the original.

And yet, beyond even this questioning, it remains to be asked whether in the case of such texts the distinction between the meaning and the so-called inner voice can remain intact, whether what one would presume to distinguish as the meaning is not already so infused with the tone, tempo, modulation, and articulation as to be inseparable from them. In this case, if the inner voice belongs to what one would have called the meaning, it would not suffice to reconstitute the task of the translator as one of preserving both meaning and the various moments that go to make up the inner voice. One could not keep the classical determination of translation, of its norm or ideal, intact simply by adding the requirement that other moments supplementary to meaning be pre-

67. Ibid., 284.

served along with the meaning. And just as the inherence of the inner voice in what comes to be said has the effect of putting the classical determination of translation in question, it also suspends the very determination of discourse as expression of meaning, as expression that is distinct from—that does not itself belong to—the meaning it expresses. What would also be put in question—that is, reopened to questioning—are those translations that constitute the manifold within which discourse and translation in its alleged proper sense operate. It would be a matter, then, of taking up again the original complication outlined by Aristotle, of doing so in such a way as to reopen those questions that have almost always seemed to have been settled by Aristotle. It would be a matter of unsettling and reinterrogating the way in which words are signs of what the Greeks called affections in the soul and the latter, in turn, likenesses of things.

In his deconstructive studies of Husserl's *Logical Investigations*, Derrida has demonstrated how meaning as the correlate of a pure intention is necessarily contaminated by what belongs inseparably to its expression, by what Derrida calls indication (*l'indice*).[68] To this extent he reopens questioning at the level of the original complication outlined by Aristotle; Derrida pursues such questioning most openly—though by no means exclusively—in his deconstruction of phonocentrism, calling into question—indeed inverting and displacing—the relation that Aristotle posits in declaring that written words are symbols of spoken words. Derrida also focuses quite precisely on what the contamination of meaning entails with regard to translation: "Within the limits in which it is possible, in which at least it *appears* possible, translation practices the difference between signified and signifier. But if this difference is never pure, no more so is translation, and for the notion of translation it would be necessary to substitute a notion of *transformation*: regulated transformation of one language by another, of one text by another. We will never have, and in fact have never had, to do with some 'transport' of pure signifieds from one lan-

68. Derrida, *La Voix et le Phénomène* (Paris: Presses Universitaires de France, 1967), chaps. 1–3; see my discussion in *Double Truth* (Albany: State University of New York Press, 1995), chap. 1.

guage to another, or within one and the same language, that the signifying instrument—or 'vehicle'—would leave virgin and untouched."[69]

Meaning is not left virgin and untouched either as the pure correlate of an intentional act or as sequestered from what belongs to its expression (for instance, the inner voice). Translation cannot, then, consist in the transposition of meaning from one language to another; it cannot consist simply in the movement from a signifier in one language, through the meaning, to a signifier in the other language. Even if translation and the lawful play of imagination that animates it must still in a sense go through this movement, the movement alone as pure transposition will no longer, as in the classical determination, suffice to define translation. Rather, in passing between languages, the play of imagination will produce a regulated transformation. As when, with the translation of *Bottom* as *Zettel*, the connection with weaving remains invariant while the association with the creature with whose head Bottom is endowed is exchanged for an association with the writing and production of plays.

For all its radicality, Benjamin's analysis stops short of drawing these conclusions. Benjamin fully recognizes that mere restitution such as would produce likeness (that is, similarity of meaning) between translation and original is insufficient: "it can be demonstrated that no translation would be possible if in its ultimate essence it strove for likeness [*Ähnlichkeit*] to the original."[70] While there are of course good reasons for this, the "demonstration" that Benjamin offers, at least immediately, is almost beside the point: he refers to the changes in tenor and significance that the original undergoes over time as a result of general changes in the language and to the comparable changes sustained by the translation as a result of transformations occurring in the language of the translator, transformations that may even be determined in part by great translations. While one will grant that consequently the relation between the original and the translation will undergo a change, it

69. Derrida, *Positions* (Paris: Les Éditions de Minuit, 1972), 31.
70. Benjamin, "Die Aufgabe des Übersetzers," 53.

will nonetheless need to be maintained that their relation can change only if there is a determinate relation, some accord between translation and original that—whatever future changes may occur—will have been aimed at in producing the translation.

In any case Benjamin's point is only that the relation between translation and original is not one of likeness or similarity. What, then, is the character of their relation? Benjamin sometimes proposes a phenomenological strategy in order to explicate this relation. The task of the translator would be to recover the intention of the original so as to reenact that intention within the language in which the translation is to be produced: "The task of the translator consists in finding that intention in the language into which he is translating that awakens in that language the echo of the original."[71] Yet an echo is a kind of imperfect likeness, and it is thus on the intention, not the echo it produces, that Benjamin must insist. Thus: "A translation, instead of making itself similar to the meaning of the original, must lovingly and in detail form within its own language the way of meaning [*Art des Meinens*] belonging to the original. . . ."[72] Up to this point Benjamin's position does not differ essentially from Gadamer's in *Truth and Method*: translation is a matter of reenacting the meaning of the original in another language, recontextualizing one and the same meaning or at least the intention to which it corresponds. But Benjamin turns in a very different direction in the continuation of the sentence: ". . . thus making both the original and the translation recognizable as fragments of a greater language, just as shards are fragments of a vessel." What connects original and translation Benjamin calls kinship (*Verwandtschaft*), a kinship between the language of the original and that of the translation. It is in his explication of this kinship that Benjamin explains his reference to a

71. Ibid., 57.

72. Ibid., 59. The recourse to the intention rather than directly to the meaning is expressed perhaps most succinctly in the following passage: "On the other hand, over against the meaning, the language of the translation can—indeed must—let itself go, in order to give voice to the *intentio* of the original, not as reproduction [*Wiedergabe*] but as harmony, as a supplement to the language in which the original is expressed, as its own kind of *intentio*" (ibid.).

"greater language" of which original and translation would be recognizable as fragments. He declares that this kinship of languages consists in the fact "that in each of them as a whole one and the same thing is meant [*gemeint*], which however is attainable by no single one of them but only by the totality of their intentions supplementing each other: pure language."[73] Translation would, then, actualize this kinship, integrating languages, bringing them into a certain correspondence in their way of meaning, ripening the seed of pure language.

From this point on, Benjamin's analysis breaks radically with the classical determination of translation and even with its hermeneutic modification. He is acutely aware of the danger of breaking all bonds of translation to the restitution of meaning. He writes of how the task of ripening the seed of pure language "seems never resolvable." He asks—not just rhetorically—whether the very ground of translation does not withdraw "once the restitution of meaning ceases to provide the measure." And he concludes: "Viewed negatively, this is indeed the meaning of all the foregoing."[74] Thus, Benjamin does not conceal the consequences that must be faced once one abandons restitution of meaning as the measure of translation and instead dedicates translation to the task of ripening the seed of pure language.

And yet, for all its radicality, this move does not break entirely with the classical determination of translation. In the end, as the end to which all translation would—even if without determinate measure—be referred, Benjamin's analysis invokes pure meaning such as would remain uncontaminated by signifying operations. This pure meaning, virgin and untouched, is no longer (as in the classical determination) that which can be said (signified) in any particular language but rather is, in a very classical sense, the ideal, that which all languages together, with their mutually supplementary intentions, would say if that totality of signification were, at the limit, to be realized. Thus, Benjamin's analysis posits at the ideal limit a totality of meaning that would have escaped contami-

73. Ibid., 54.
74. Ibid., 58.

nation by signification, a realm of meaning in which all communication and even all intentions are extinguished, a pure language in which there remains only the expressionless word.

Benjamin declares that "the task of the translator is to release [*erlösen*—hence also: save, rescue] in his own language that pure language that is captivated by another, to liberate the language imprisoned in a work in his recasting of the work."[75] One cannot but wonder: Is language imprisoned in works so as to be in need of being liberated? Or does it only seem imprisoned because the language of and in the work is regarded from the vantage point of the ideal of pure meaning, of pure language? Is it not rather in a work that language is liberated, freed to itself in such a way that what has not—and perhaps could not have—been previously said comes to be said? In any case there is every reason to wonder—as indeed does Benjamin himself—how translation governed only by reference to such an ideal of pure meaning and by the imperative of liberating it could be regulated. Could ripening the seed of pure language ever become—or be assured of becoming—a regulated transformation?

The radical critique of the classical determination of translation, which with Nietzsche takes the form of mere inversion, becomes with Benjamin a rupture, a break. Or rather, it would have been a break, an utter break, had it not reconstituted the classical determination at the limit, as an ideal, retaining—even if at an unbridgeable distance—a vestige of pure meaning. If translation is, then, from this distance, liberation of pure meaning, giving it back to itself—that is, still, restitution of meaning—mere reference to this ideal does not suffice to prevent translation from becoming capricious (or, at best, creative) transformation.

If one is to persist in the deconstruction of the classical determination while also redetermining translation as regulated transformation, as engaged by lawful play of imagination, then it is imperative to turn back from the dream of pure language, which is also a dream of nontranslation. It is imperative to be attentive, not to a remote vestige of meaning by which translation would—but

75. Ibid., 60.

cannot—be bound, but to what bounds and is bound to language as it operates in human comportment. Once language is no longer construed simply as signification, as a totality of signifiers signifying meanings themselves independent of signification, then what bounds and is bound to language proves to be nothing other than what comes to be said—*das, was zur Sprache kommt*. What comes to be said in speech or in a linguistic work is nothing other than that which the speech or the linguistic work makes manifest, that which it lets—in the unique way proper to language—show itself, come to presence. This is what, bound to language and its manifestive force, also bounds language, determines its bounds, reflects back to it its very determinateness. If translation of speech or of a linguistic work is to be a transformation that is regulated, if it is to be engaged by a play of imagination that is lawful, then reference to—that is, being bound by—that which the speech or work makes manifest is imperative.

It would be a matter of attending again to the force of words and of bringing translation again to rely on the force of words—on their force of making manifest—in order to bring into play a measure by which to regulate translation. By being bound by what the original makes manifest, translation would carry out a regulated transformation of the original.

As in the rendering of *fancy's images* as *Spiel der Einbildung* in which Schlegel will have been attentive to the way in which Shakespeare's play makes imagination manifest and will, by introducing *Spiel*, have enhanced the manifestive force in the translation in a way that accords with the original.

Four *Varieties of Untranslatability*

Attestations to untranslatability abound. Poetry especially, many have declared, is untranslatable. Yet translations of poetry also abound. Even the poetry of those whose poetic gift and artistic mastery would seem to make their work—if any is indeed—untranslatable has found translators, and the best among them have produced translations that no one would deem unworthy of the title. At least with only rare exceptions: Hölderlin's translations of Sophocles were dismissed by his contemporaries, largely because of what they saw as a monstrously literal rendering of the syntax of the original. But such an exception only serves to point to a depth of translatability that could be fathomed only by such a poet as Hölderlin, that could only have remained otherwise concealed. While Hölderlin remained unheeded as a translator by those whom one would most have expected to have recognized his gift and his mastery as a translator (Hegel, for instance), his incomparable achievement was eventually to come to light. More than a century later Benjamin writes of Hölderlin's translations of *Oedipus Tyrannus* and *Antigone*: "In them the harmony of the languages is so profound that sense is touched by language only as an aeolian harp is touched by the wind. Hölderlin's translations are prototypes of their kind; they are to even the most perfect renderings of their texts as a prototype is to a model [*als das Urbild zum Vorbild*]."[1]

Poetry is not, then, simply untranslatable, not even the poetry of Sophocles, of Shakespeare, of Hölderlin himself. It is not untranslatable in an unconditional sense: there is no poem of which one can say in advance that every would-be translation of it will prove disentitled as such, will prove to be unentitled to be called a translation. If, nonetheless, attestations to the untranslatability of

1. Benjamin, "Die Aufgabe des Übersetzers," 61.

poetry abound, what is attested can only be a more limited untranslatability. In whatever way the attestations are framed, regardless of how unconditionally they may be stated, the untranslatability of poetry thus attested can consist only in poetry's not being translatable without loss and without the flattening and distortion generally that is produced by such loss. Yet, at least in the case of the best translations, a certain gain also is brought about, certain enhancements of the original, which may offset or otherwise balance what is lost through the reductions, transpositions, and shifts that translation requires. Even—perhaps most of all—in the case of poetry, translation is a matter of exchange; it operates within an economy geared to the difference between the two languages, an economy that is not fixed but is open to the initiatives of an adventurous translator, one willing to venture a certain expenditure with confidence of what will be returned. Such initiative may open up a hitherto unsuspected depth of translatability, as in the case of Hölderlin's translations of Sophocles. But it may also fail abysmally. For it is not just a matter of willingness to venture nor of confidence in one's venture; in the case of one such as Hölderlin the utmost reticence may be in play. It is a matter of the translator's gift, of his genius for opening a favorable transformation between the two languages. But it is equally imperative that what occurs through the play of imagination be lawful, that the translation be a regulated transformation. Short of reconstituting the classical determination of translation, regulation can be operative only through attentiveness to what the original makes manifest, to the force of its words.

As already in the attestations regarding poetry, untranslatability can itself become a theme of speech, even to such an extent that the speech may identify, name, or mark something that cannot be said in that very speech, something untranslatable not only into that speech but into any speech whatsoever. One may, for instance, write about how what one *would* say escapes what one does—indeed can—say. In such a case one writes about the untranslatable, supplementing what one writes with a writing that testifies to a certain untranslatability operative in what one writes: as, for instance, writing in a letter of one's deep feelings for another, one writes also of the untranslatability of those feelings into writing; that is, one attests in the writing to their untranslatability into writing.

The configuration of such untranslatability is quite different from the untranslatability of a text in one language into another language. For what is attested when one writes of the untranslatability of certain feelings is an untranslatability that, while necessarily not total, is nonetheless unconditional. It is not merely that if one's feelings were to be translated, to be expressed in words, there would be a certain loss, as when Plato's translators render φάρμακον as poison, losing sight of the medicinal effect for which in his final words Socrates expresses his debt to Asclepius. In the case of untranslatable feelings it is such that—or at least it is attested to be such that—any would-be translation of those feelings into speech would be not just a bad translation, not just a translation in which much would be lost, but rather no translation at all. Any alleged expression of those feelings in language would prove to be an imposter, something quite other than an expression of those feelings. And yet, the very possibility of attesting to such untranslatability requires that it not be total: in order to identify, name, mark the feelings as untranslatable into speech, it must be possible to say something about them and so to mark a limit of their untranslatability. It must be possible at least to name them, to call them by some such name as *feelings*; and it must be possible at least to say of them that they are untranslatable. Because at least their untranslatability is translatable into speech, it cannot be total.

Yet attestation of untranslatability, of unconditional untranslatability, is not limited to writing or to language generally. It is not only in language, not only by way of language, that one can attest to an untranslatability into language as such and into such meanings as can be signified by linguistic signifiers. There are indeed exceptional cases in which that which is attested to be untranslatable into linguistically signifiable meanings comes to provide the very medium of the attestation. In such cases there is a peculiar coincidence of attestation with that to the untranslatability of which it attests. As in the case of a painter who paints in such a way as to attest in the painting to its untranslatability into language, into what can be said.

Focusing now on such a case, it will be a matter of again trans-

1. Mimmo Paladino. *Senza titolo* [Untitled], 1989. Oil on canvas and wood, 108 × 88 × 15 cm.

lating *translation* beyond translation within a language or between languages, of translating translation and the questions it prompts to the interval, the difference, separating language and all that language can say from painting and all the elements of visibility as such that painting can visibly present.

In 1990 the celebrated Italian artist Mimmo Paladino exhibited at Villa delle Rose in Bologna a cycle of seven paintings along with a cycle of eight closely related drawings.[2] The two cycles were given the single title EN DO RE. One of the paintings (see figure 1) has on its surface an inscription that is almost the same as this title; the title given to the two cycles, EN DO RE, is, by Paladino's own testimony,[3] merely a mutation of the inscription in the painting, EN DE RE. In addition to clarifying the relation between the title and the inscription, Paladino made available a small book entitled EN DE RE, a very strange book about which it suffices here to say only that it disrupts every attempt to translate—and so to

2. There is a catalogue to the exhibition: *Paladino* (Bologna: Nuova Alfa Editoriale, 1990). See also the volume of reproductions and essays entitled EN DO RE (Siracusa: Tema Celeste Edizioni, 1990).

3. Mimmo Paladino, letter to author, 30 August 1994.

make sense of—these enigmatic marks EN DE RE.[4] Thus, when EN DE RE is actually inscribed in the painting, one should not assume that Paladino is producing some kind of synthesis of word and image; for what look like words are not words, that is, are not translatable into words. Paladino refers to them—undecidably—as ciphers (*cifra*).

Though the cycle of paintings has the cipher-title *EN DO RE*, sharing it with the cycle of drawings, the individual paintings in the cycle are untitled, are designated as *Senza titolo*. This disentitlement could be regarded as a shield meant to secure a pure visibility, to guard the paintings against any intrusion by language, to forestall all translation of the visible into the word. Addressed to the viewer as a kind of warning, the disentitlement would be, in this case, the painter's way of prescribing that one behold the paintings as they display themselves before one's vision, leaving aside all translation of the spectacle into discourse, which could only contaminate the pure visibility of the paintings. By withholding titles from the paintings, the painter would seem to proclaim a reign of absolute untranslatability, an untranslatability by which the paintings would be sealed off in themselves over against the otherwise intrusive word; disentitlement would, in this case, absolve the paintings in their visible presence from all relation whatsoever to language.

And yet, disentitlement is not itself totally absolved from language: when works not only are deprived of a title but also are presented, in exhibitions and catalogues, with the designation *untitled*, such disentitlement borders on entitling them, on entitling them to the title *untitled*. Yet the very sense of the designation *untitled* requires that it not be a title: a painting can be designated as *untitled* only if it has no title. One would thus have to say that the designation *untitled* both is and is not a title; or rather, that it is a title the very bestowal of which frees the painting from entitlement. With this designation it is as though language only grazed the surface of the painting, being reflected back to itself rather

---

4. Achille Bonito Oliva with Mimmo Paladino, *EN DE RE* (Modena: Emilio Mazzoli Editore, 1980). See my discussion of this book in *Shades—Of Painting at the Limit* (Bloomington: Indiana University Press, 1998), 120–24.

than adhering to the painting, letting the painting thus go free. Here language outdistances itself. Yet, in such disentitlement, the painting will have been grazed by the word, will have been released by self-outdistancing language. As also through the inscription of untranslatable ciphers, the painting will have been touched by language. But rather than importing language, as it were, into the painting, the effect is to take up, in a painterly way, the question of language and painting, the question of the translatability and untranslatability of painting.

In disentitlement the painting is touched by language only to be released to itself, to its pure visibility, its pure untranslatability. This untranslatability is not absolute: The painting is not absolved from all relation to language, since the disentitling word is precisely what frees the painting to itself and lets its pure visibility be sheltered from the intrusion of language. Disentitling is a way of saying the untranslatability of the painting, of translating its untranslatability while leaving the painting nonetheless untranslated, indeed untranslatable. One will want to ask: What is its untranslatability?—and yet, the question is possible only if, in asking about the *what*, the question outdistances itself and releases the painting from the hold of anything like a *what*. Only in this way, by turning language back to itself so as to free from it that of which one will have spoken, can one say what the untranslatability of painting is: that the visible elements gathered in their visibility in the painting cannot be translated into a linguistically signifiable meaning or complex of meanings such as could be configured in a title or in a discourse elaborating the sense of a title. To be sure, the painting is touched by language and its significations: in being disentitled, in bearing an inscription of quasi-linguistic ciphers, even in being written about by the artist. And yet, it is touched by language only to be released into a silence that can never be matched by words. What constitutes its untranslatability is this silence.

Even in the case of paintings that are not disentitled, paintings to which Paladino gives a title, there operates still a certain releasement from language, a certain reign (even though not absolute) of untranslatability. For, by the artist's testimony, his titles are not such as to subsume the painting under a governing signification: "I never give titles that convey a particular meaning, which could trap one into reading the work in strictly literary and symbolic terms." Instead, writes Paladino, "The title of a work always represents for me the side that is disquieting [or: displacing—*il lato spiazzante*] for the interpretation of the work."[5] The title, one could say, serves precisely to disturb, interrupt, and displace all interpretation oriented to replacing the work's visible presentation with linguistic significations; it serves to block—to secure the painting against—all hermeneutical efforts to translate visibility into signification.

This is nowhere more transparently the case than in those instances where *silence* or *silent* belongs to the title. There are several such titles: a painting from 1977 is entitled *Silence, I am retiring to paint* (*Silenzioso, mi ritiro a dipingere*); two others from 1979 and 1980, respectively, bear the same remarkable title *Silent Red* (*Rosso silenzioso*).[6] As the word *silence*, when uttered, breaks the very silence to which it refers, so in these titles the word, reflected back to itself, frees the paintings to their silence, says and yet releases their untranslatability. Most forcefully so when *silent* is conjoined with the name of something distinctively visible, with a name such as *red*: the red that is painted—as in the two paintings entitled *Silent Red*—is not the red that can be said; it is a red that is only to be seen, a silent red.

As with the indescribable red of an Aegean sunset. Or the unspeakably beautiful red of a rose. One senses somehow that such sights are to be beheld in silence. One senses, no matter what one may say, that they are untranslatable.

What is perhaps most remarkable about the paintings (and indeed the drawings too) in the cycle bearing the cipher-title EN

---

5. Mimmo Paladino, letter to author, January 1991.

6. The 1979 work entitled *Silent Red* is reproduced in Achille Bonito Oliva with Mimmo Paladino, *EN DE RE*, 37; as is *Silence, I am retiring to paint* (ibid., 15). The latter, as well as *Silent Red* from 1980, is included in the catalogue of the Villa delle Rosa exhibition. Both are reproduced also in *Paladino: una monografia / a monograph* (Milan: Charta, 2001), 65, 90; this retrospective collection also includes images of several related works: two from 1979 entitled *Silence* (*Silenzioso*) (ibid., 76, 79) and another from 1978 designated *Untitled* (*Senza titolo*) (ibid., 68), which resembles the 1980 *Silent Red* in showing an only slightly interrupted field of red.

2. Mimmo Paladino. *Senza titolo* [Untitled], 1989. Oil on canvas and wood, 108 × 88 × 15 cm.

DO RE is the way in which the release, the withdrawal, that belongs to painting as such is set into the work itself. Each of the paintings has a double structure (see figure 2): there is a lower surface over which is placed an obfuscating panel, which conceals a portion of the lower surface and whatever images may be depicted on that surface. In most of the paintings—or rather, works, for the double structure makes them exceed painting—there are also images on the obfuscating panels. As a result of this double structure and the artistic handling of it, there is in each case set into the work a withdrawal of images, a retreating of images behind other images. In other words—as if words were not precisely the issue—the work gathers and distributes the images in such a way as to present their disappearance, their escape from view. In this way the works present the painterly analogue of their own untranslatability: as the images escape from view and are presented in the work as escaping from view, so the painting itself, that is, what is presented in the painting, escapes from words. Even—it must be said—from the very words in which it has just been said. By presenting the disappearance of images, the painted work also presents—in the only way it could be presented in a painted work, in the very element of painting and thus necessarily only by outdistancing itself, as from the other side language outdistances itself—the untranslatability that belongs to the painted work.

In the case of painting, untranslatability does not have to do, then, with linguistic difference, with the difference between languages in which one would—but cannot—say the same, that is, speak tautologically. It has to do, rather, with the difference between language and the visible; more precisely (though still classically), it has to do with the relation—or nonrelation—between linguistically signifiable meanings and configurations of the visible in which the visible is brought to present its very visibility. Ultimately, this untranslatability has to do with the very difference that Socrates opened up—and opened to questioning—when he ventured his second sailing, turning from visibly present things to λόγοι. One could call this the difference of all differences, the gigantic difference, recalling that it was this difference, the question of this difference, that provoked the contention described in Plato's *Sophist* as a γιγαντομαχία περὶ τῆς οὐςίας. Western philosophy was eventually to domesticate this difference in a series of translations of the words νοητόν and αἰσθητόν, thereby stabilizing also the sense of translation, giving it its classical determination. If it is only since Nietzsche that philosophy has learned again how to open this difference to questioning, painting can also attest—has perhaps always attested—to its questionableness, to its utter irreducibility, to the untranslatability that separates what, nonetheless and most remarkably, are called by the same name: *sense*.

Music would attest even more forcefully, if it were possible, to the untranslatability of sense into sense: the impossibility of saying in words what is sounded in a musical composition is so patent as to be proverbial. Thus music would add its voice to that by which philosophy would open to questioning anew the gigantic difference between—and as the difference between—that which is made manifest through the force of words and that which can be seen, heard, or otherwise sensed.

And yet, the case of music is different. For however untranslatable music may be into words, music can be and often is put into words; perhaps even in an originary way music is linked to song, to the human voice. Without weakening in the least the utter untranslatability of music into words, one will need to say that nonetheless there is a certain affinity between music and words, especially between music and such words as can be sung, namely, poetry. In their untranslatable difference, music and poetry have a profound affinity and can come together in an accord that is mutually enhancing.

Kant caught a glimpse of this affinity. In the *Critique of Judgment* he links fine art to the expression of aesthetic ideas and as a result divides the fine arts according to the analogy between the arts and the way expression functions in speech. Taking linguistic expression to consist of the three moments, word, gesture, and tone, Kant divides the fine arts, accordingly, into arts of speech (poetry and oratory), arts corresponding to gesture (the visual/formative arts—*die bildenden Künste*), and those corresponding to tone, which for Kant are arts of the play of sensations. Music falls in this third group. What music shares with speech, hence with poetry, is thus tone, and it is in their respective tones that music and poetry have an affinity. Kant writes: "Every linguistic expression has in its context a tone appropriate to its meaning." One could say: within language, within poetry in particular, there is always already something like music, a kind of protomusic. Within language there is always already another language, an untranslatable language of tones. Music lets this other language sound outside poetry and its proper language: "the art of music employs this language all by itself in its full force."[7]

There is a further consequence, one that could also be reached by another route quite independent of Kant's systematic considerations (which in other regards have the effect of ranking music as the lowest of the fine arts or even as not quite a fine art). The consequence can be stated thus: music is always already mixed into poetry, always already inherent in it, and for this reason music can come to supplement poetry. Despite the untranslatability that separates music decisively from poetry, the art of music can let sound outside poetry the very music, the protomusic, the language of tones, inherent in a poetic work; and thereby, without violat-

7. Kant, *Kritik der Urteilskraft*, §53.

ing the immediate untranslatability, it can supplement the poetic work—can, in another, more profound sense of this word, translate it.

As in the Overture and Incidental Music that Mendelssohn composed for *A Midsummer Night's Dream*. As in the Scherzo's musical presentation of the world of the fairies. As in the eerie chromatic Andante's setting the tone for Oberon's and Puck's casting of the spell and in its later inversion as Oberon undoes the spell upon Titania. As in the parody funeral march's matching perfectly in tone the scene of the performance of "Pyramus and Thisbe." As in the Nocturne's sounding of the wood's magic and of the depth of the lover's sleep. As in the musical interlude that transports the listening spectator from the scene of Hermia's frantic search for Lysander to that of the entrance of the mechanicals, when, as if to the jocular tune heard, they arrive at the "green plot" that is to be their stage, among them, soon to be translated, Nick Bottom the weaver.

General Index

Actualitas, 17
Aeschines, 65
Aristotle, 48–50, 106
Artwork, 33–34, 80n; in Kant, 13n. *See also* Painting
Aufgabe, 18
Ausdruck, 24

Benjamin, Walter, 15–16, 80n, 88, 107–10, 112
Boswell, James, 81–82
Brann, Kalkavage, Salem, 77, 78, 79, 92

Chalcidius, 5
Cicero, 23n, 65–67
Ciphers, 116; in Paladino, 116, 118–20
Classical determination of translation, xi, 51, 62–71, 98; in Samuel Johnson, 83; limit of, 71–73; origin of, 120; and the protoclassical determination, 59–62
Colonialism, 10
Comedy, 37; in Plato's *Cratylus*, 63
Croce, Benedetto, 104

Definition: in Locke, 68–70
Demosthenes, 65
Dent, R. W., 38n
Derrida, Jacques, 4n, 34, 47, 106–107
Drama, 19, 33–37; in *A Midsummer Night's Dream*, 30, 31–32

Figal, Günter, 97
Force of imagination, 36–37, 98–99; in Schlegel, 94–98, 99–100, 110–11
Force of names (τὴν τῶν ὀνομάτων δύναμιν), 110–11, 113; in the classical determination, 62–65; in Plato's *Critias*, 55, 57–59; in Cicero, 65–67; in Locke, 67–71; of Greek words, 16–18; in music, 120–22
Fowler, Harold North, 76n, 78, 91n
Freud, Sigmund, 7–9

Gadamer, Hans-Georg, 32–34, 71–73, 88, 89, 98, 103–105
Globalization, 6

Hackforth, Reginald, 76, 78, 91
Hegel, G. W. F., 3, 16, 17, 80n, 103
Heidegger, Martin, 5–6, 17–19, 34, 72n, 84, 101–102
Highlighting (*Überhellung*), 72–79, 104

Indication (*l'indice*), 106

Jakobson, Roman, 23, 46–47, 50, 83–84
Johnson, Samuel, 80–83

Kant, Immanuel, 1–2, 13–15, 98, 99n, 121
Kirwan, Christopher, 10n

Language: Greek understanding of, 64–65; "pure" language (Benjamin), 108–109
Leibniz, Gottfried Wilhelm von, 9–13, 15, 16
Locke, John, 67–71
Locus, 5

Materia, 12
Measure, 50, 111; loss of (in Benjamin), 109–10; "radical" measures, 17–18; in the *Critias*, 51, 58–59; and imagination, 99
Music, xii, 120–22

Nachbildung, 72, 103
Nature, 68n; in Kant, 14; in Locke, 68n
Nietzsche, Friedrich, 24–25, 62, 86–87, 110, 120
Nizolius, Marius, 11

Painting, xii, 114–20
Pannwitz, Rudolph, 88
Phonocentrism, 106
Poetry: Solon's (in *Critias*), 55, 59; transla-

tion of, 17, 64, 80–81ff., 84–85, 88, 105, 112–14, 121–22
Polysemy, 22, 25, 46; of ὄνομα, 54
Proper names, 28, 47–48, 85, 92
Psychoanalysis, 7–9

Quintilian, 35

Restitution of meaning, 64; in Benjamin, 107–10; in Cicero, 67; in Gadamer's hermeneutics, 71, 104–105; impossibility of, 83–85; in Samuel Johnson, 83; in Schlegel, 95

Schlegel, August Wilhelm, 28–30, 48, 73–75, 84ff., 92–97, 99–100, 111
Schleiermacher, Friedrich, 76, 78, 91
Selbstbestand, 12
Semantic displacement, 15
Substantia, 12
Suiectum, 5
Synonym, 70

Taylor, Thomas, 5
Technology, 7
Transfero, 23, 29
Translation: as betrayal, 72, 104; as conveyance, 31; as entrancing, 28; as handing-down (*Überlieferung*), 17; history of the word, 22–23; as interpretation, 7–9, 21, 23, 29, 118; into another language, 28; as change in medium, 30; nonreciprocity, 100–101, 102–103; overtranslation, 101–103; in theatre, 19–20, 27–31, 37–45; and thinking, 18–19; as transformation, 15–17, 27, 88, 101, 106–108, 110–11, 113
Translatus, 23
Tredennick, Hugh, 77, 91

Überhellung, 72, 104
Überlieferung, 17
Unverborgenheit, 18
Unwesen, 12

Voss, Johann Heinrich, 16

Wardy, Robert, 10n
Will to power, 17

Greek Word Index

αἰσθητόν / νοητόν, 62
ἀλήθεια, 18
γράμματα, γραφόμενα, 48, 64
δεύτερος πλοῦς, 91–92
διαλέγεσθαι, 2
διάνοια, 60, 71; as "meaning," 63
διανοεῖσθαι, 2
διαπυνθάνομαι, 57
δύναμις, 67
εἰκασία, 36
εἶναι, 18
ἐνέργεια, 17
ἔργον, 35
θεωρία, 22
θυμός, 79
ἰδέα, 17, 71
λόγος, 2, 35, 49, 101
μεταφέρω, 24
ὄν, 18
ὄνομα, 49, 54, 64
πράξις, 22
ῥῆμα, 49
τέχνη, 34, 38
ὑποκείμενον, 5
φάρμακον, 76–77
χώρα, 5, 53–54

JOHN SALLIS is Edwin Erle Sparks Professor of Philosophy at Pennsylvania State University. His previous books include *Force of Imagination: The Sense of the Elemental*; *Chorology: On Beginning in Plato's* Timaeus; *Shades—Of Painting at the Limit*; *Being and Logos: Reading the Platonic Dialogues*; *Double Truth*; *Stone*; *Delimitations*; *Crossings: Nietzsche and the Space of Tragedy*; *Echoes: After Heidegger*; *Spacings—Of Reason and Imagination*; *The Gathering of Reason*; and *Phenomenology and the Return to Beginnings*.